"MAMA, 'BABE' AND ME"

Eddie Marie Jones Durham

Order this book online at www.trafford.com
or email orders@trafford.com

Most Trafford titles are also available at major online book retailers.

Printed in the United States of America.

ISBN: 978-1-4269-4033-0 (sc)
ISBN: 978-1-4269-4035-4 (e)

Library of Congress Control Number: 2010918807

Trafford rev. 03/03/2011

www.trafford.com

North America & international
toll-free: 1 888 232 4444 (USA & Canada)
phone: 250 383 6864 ♦ fax: 812 355 4082

Contents

"Mama Babe"

History is a record of what was done in the past.
It is an account of most things included, from first to last.
Things we remember, including things about which you want to say, "I forgot.
There are actions, happenings, and deeds we cherish and others we do not.
In every family things happen, we think highly of, and want everyone to know
And a lot of stuff we strongly, wish just weren't even so.
We wonder about the folks in our lineage, the ones here before we came
Wonder what they did, what they were like or what they were called, by name.
These are the questions we all are inclined to ask.
*But, trying to gather all that information can, for someone be a **real** task.*

~~~~~~~

"Mama, Mama, is dead? Mama is dead!"

"Are they sure?"

"What are we going to do with Mama gone?" These are the thoughts that went through my head when I learned that my dear, sweet mama was no longer with us.

I had been all ready registered to attend a conference in Corpus Christi, Texas. I just sat there numbly for some time. I kept having these disturbing thoughts. "My Mama is gone! What am I going to do? Why did Mama Have to go?

The questions didn't go away after the funeral. They would only get worse when I would visit Laura's, my sister where Mama stayed for the last more than twenty years of her life.

I still expect to see Mama when I went there. After a while I decided to put together all the things I could gather on Mama's life and the lives she touched while she sojourned on this side. Her life was such an example of God's grace, in granting one person the strength to be the person she was. Thinking of her and trying to organize her life history is a help and maybe a hindrance too. It keeps her close as I let my mind refresh loving memories. I have learned a few things about her that I didn't know while she was alive.

I wanted to begin at the beginning, but pulling Mama's background together including her parents, grandparents, great-grandparents and others, has proven to be quite a problem, because so many of the people I needed to get the information from are already dead and gone too. I decided to have talks with as many members of the family and others who knew something about the things I wanted to include. These were people who knew people were "in the know" before they also died.

My gathering of Mama's background history, her three husbands and, the families her life touched, is a real engaging experience. That is bringing not only information but deeper feelings for many family members.

I'd like to show how Mama; Nayme Everlena "Babe" Hayes Weaver Jones Durham, influenced my life and the lives of other family members as well. Not all of her background histories I wanted are obtainable. Yet, I decided to make an attempt to put as much together in this write-up, as I could and as well as a bit of something just about me.

Mama had three husbands, Austin "Butch" Weaver, Will Dexter Jones and Luke Durham. I decided to include as much of their family history, and as many of their family members I was able to get the information for. This I did for grandchildren, great grands and future generations that would have the desire to know something about their history.

My view of Mama's life was that she was a God fearing, gracious, hard working wife and loving mother who was determined to do God's will in every way she knew how. She depended on Him, GOD, and His Word. She had to be a woman of tremendous courage and stamina who withstood much in her life. Her strong belief in God helped her to survive. I know she could not have done it without the strength, and guidance, of the gracious God she pointed us, her children, too. She demonstrated it for all of us and all others who got to know her, with the life she lived before us and, by her steadfast faith in this loving God.

I will begin this record with her grandparents who had to have been slaves. Wade and Laura Collins, Great-Grandpa Wade and Great-Grandma Laura produced two girls, Ella Bruce (in 1881), and Angie and two brothers, Melvin, "Pal", and DeWitt Collins.

Grandma Laura **I** got to know for a little while. But, by the time I came along Grandpa Wade had already passed away. In Grandma Laura, one saw a very proud woman with determination and stamina. (When I think of her propensity for wearing high heel shoes, I think maybe, I think I inherited some of her **good** qualities.)

I know that she had a good affect on Mama, because I think much of her stamina came from the training and love she received from Grandma Laura. The visits we made to Grandma Laura's home were happy, informative experiences.

She told us one day we were visiting, "You know ya'll are real lucky children. Both your Mama and your Daddy are out there with you."

"Why does that make us so lucky, Grandma Laura?"

"Cause y'all still have both of your parents. I had to be there to see mine being sold when I was small. I never got to see them anymore. Yeah I'd say you are lucky."

"What was that like Grandma, Laura?"

"Honey, you don't want to know that. Besides I have this food ready for the family."

I don't remember her telling us too much more about her life because we just had fun playing when we were there. Her history was not what was on our minds at that early age.

I feel that Grandma Laura had a hard time coming through this horrid experience from the comments she made then, and I feel there were many others she did not tell us about. Yet she did come through it all with pride, and a strong will to do good things for everyone. She seemed to have been the kind of person, she believed God, wanted her to be.

I knew, and was impressed by Grandma Laura but, I have no information about what Grandpa Wade was like, nor do I remember anyone talking about him. These persons were our maternal grandparents.

We were told of Mama's fraternal grandparents, Frank and Liza Hayes, who were the parents of Isaiah Hayes, our grandfather. If he had siblings I have not been made privy to that knowledge.

Isaiah Hayes and Ella Bruce Collins, my grandmother, married somewhere along the way. To their union on May 3, 1910 a baby girl they named Nayme Everlena was born after her two other sisters: Lellure Jane, born July 24, 1902, Arlena who was born December 3, 1909. They had two brothers, J. P and Artis Hayes whose birth information I have no knowledge of.

Mama's sister Arlean got the nickname "Sis," and somewhere along the way Mama became known by the nickname of "Babe."(I have a feeling it was because she was the youngest child of the family.)

Babe is what family, friends and acquaintances always called her. She was called by that name until her death. She was known as Aunt Babe, Cousin Babe, Miss Babe and even Grandma Babe, later by her grandchildren and one or two friends of ours.

She stopped using her first name as a child, and I doubt that even many family members even knew it was part of her name until her death and it was placed on her funeral program. None of them had ever heard before.

Grandpa Isaiah and Big Mama, (to Mama's children,) and Mama Ella, (to her other grandchildren) had four lovely children. They didn't stay married to each other. Their marriage was dissolved. After its dissolution, Big Mama, remarried, separated, and remarried. We believe, from the comments she made, that it at least **6** more times!

She married and lived in so many different places, even though, she had legal custody of the children, Mama and her siblings were reared by Grandma Laura. Big Mama had no stable place for herself or them. Big Mama had no more children.

I believe Big Mama's marriage history and, her frequent relocations had a lot to do with her, what one would term in today's society, illness or ailment. Without a diagnosis I will refer to it as an ailment, disorder or disease. She suffered from this ailment as long as I knew her. The term used in the Bible would have been 'one possessed by demons.'

I came up with this idea when she came over to stay with us in between her stays in the many different places she called home. During the day, she would seem just like anyone else, except at times a bit cranky or grouchy, and most of the times when quiet for a minute, sleepy. At night she changed completely. You would be sound asleep and all of a sudden you would be awakened by arguments and other noises. In the area where Big Mama was, you would also hear many voices. Some of the voices would be in a conversational tone and some quite hostile. They would be talking and yelling about all kinds of things.

It could be one frightening experience! You are sound asleep, suddenly you hear someone scream, or yell then someone talking loudly. There would then seem to be two or three voices in a heated exchange! Yet you would know, that only Big Mama in the room. In the morning she would act as if nothing had gone on. The only thing you would notice was that she'd be sleepy or nodding off most of the day.

Grandpa Isaiah also married again. His second wife was Ms Alice. He did have more children. Mama gained three more sisters; Alberta, Nola, and Phoebe as well as another brother Artis Hayes. They all grew up in an area of Freestone County that is known then and today as Plum Creek. The community was on the Farm to Market Road, #489, leading from what is now Interstate 45, (which *was*, Highway 75) passing through the Shiloh/Butler Community to Highway 84 between Fairfield and Palestine, Texas at a place labeled The Crossroads.

They attended the Plum Creek Baptist Church there in the Plum Creek Community. What schooling they received was there in the Thorndale-Plum Creek Communities. However, the school regulations back then were totally different from the ones we know today. There was a lack of any laws governing the education of Black children, if there were they were not enforced, and because of it, many of the children didn't receive much in the way of an adequate education. Some of the children received none at all. Mama was only able to get through the 3rd grade. This time was so soon after the Blacks were freed that many were glad to get any education at all, even a substandard one. Many were just glad to learn how to read a bit, so many didn't ever learn to do more than sign their names. Some couldn't even do that.

What happened in their teen years I have little knowledge of, but the little I do recall her talking about was that it was very difficult. Since they were living with just the basic necessities of life much of the time one can only imagine what it was like.

I do know that Mama grew to be an attractive young woman. She was still ... when she became my mother years later. To me she was, until her demise.

MARRIAGE

There is a lovely golden bond,

That is to unite two hearts together as one

It is to enrich two lives, filling them with joy

If love, care and consideration both participants employ.

It gives each one, a person with whom to share thoughts, worries, and plans

And to share the thrills of passion or just the comfort of just holding hands

It provides a companion to walk with through the passing years

And the person who is there, in good times, bad times, through sorrows and tears

It is when one gets a soul-mate, partner, one's other half and friend

United together in matrimony hoping to love to the very end

Many become parents by the direct will of God

For some it might be quite easy and other times very hard

1ˢᵗ Husband, Austin "Butch" Weaver

Sometimes we get what we want
But find we do need what we get
When that happens to one
Heartache is a very likely the occurrence, on that you can bet!

In our culture that no matter where one is, in recent history, girls dream of the day they will fall in love and marry that special man. It is a dream almost all girls have of getting that special mate. In most girls' lives it is a much anticipated time that she looks forward to. I expect that Mama was no different from the average girl. She was probably looking forward to that date with her destiny. In central Texas where she lived, there was a Reverend Will Weaver, who was said to have been part descendent of the Choctaw Indians. The community was not far from Plum Creek. He was the father of one daughter, Golden and one son, J. W., before marrying his second wife Maggie. After marrying Mrs. Maggie, Reverend Will, as he was called by most who knew him, became the parents of Aile, Robert, and a set of twins; Missy and Austin Weaver. Austin was later nicknamed "Butch."

Reverend Will Weaver

Austin "Butch" Weaver grew to be a tall, handsome, light-brown-skinned, curly-haired young man. He met Mama somewhere along the way. He was what some of the young people today would refer to as a '**Bad** Boy.' From all indications, Mama was only about fifteen when she met and married, Butch Weaver. His mother did not approve of their marriage at all.

Their marriage did not turn into what Mama, or any other girl, for that matter would have dreamed of having. Problems developed very early, *lots of them*! Yet, in spite of those problems Mr. Butch and Mama had two handsome sons. The older boy, Otis, was born March 27, 1927 when Mama was two months short of her seventeenth birthday. Cotis, her second child was born the very next year on November 14, 1928. Mama was at this point 18 years and 7 months old. She now had two children less than two years old to take care of!

Tumultuous, was one way one could describe the relationship of Mr. Butch and Mama. They had some very serious issues. He was a husband who was not there for her most of the time from all she said. It must have been very hard for her. He would be gone for days sometimes. Her being pregnant so soon after marriage, then giving birth with only the help of a midwife, in a home with so little support, must have been quite traumatic. Especially, for one as young naive as she was then. After giving birth to the second child the very next year, it must have made for quite a bit of work, heartache and frustration. Mrs. Maggie had not approved of the marriage in the first place so, it was no surprise that Mama said that she gave her a very cold shoulder much of the time. She even received reprimands from her about one thing or another. This must have been hard to take since they all lived in the same house. One still has no idea of what kind of help she was given, but she must have gotten some, because of what happened later.

Her husband, Mr. Butch, drank excessively and while doing so was many times stayed away from home for days at a time, yet the major problem in the marriage was the physical abuse Mama received from him. When he did come home from a binge there would be even more trauma than usual. This must have made life really miserable. The exact reasons he gave for most of his physical abuse I never heard her say.

I learned the reason why she received the first beating when I overheard someone comment to Mama about how splendid her brown flour-gravy always was. She made no comment at the time of the compliments, except to smile and say, "Thank you." (This was on one of the many occasions when she was serving guests that were at our house. Because, for some reason even though it was such a small house we often had lots of company that she cooked for.)

I asked her later, "Mama how did, you learn to make the gravy so good all the time?"

Her reply was, "I learned to do it well because Butch, beat me until I knew how to do it that way. When I first married him, I knew how to 'raise a gravy' with meat while smothering it, but he wanted it alone. He wanted gravy with nothing in it!

"So the making of this type of gravy brought on me as I said, the first beating. It was by no means the last."

Mama's and Mr. Butch's marriage was short. They separated when Otis was three years old and Cotis was only two. I have speculated that since they were in the home with her in-laws, Rev. Will and Mrs. Maggie is why Mama left the boys. I do know that when they separated she did not get to see them afterward for years! They then stayed with Mrs. Maggie, and were reared by her.

She probably just wanted to be out of harm's way since she was running from Mr. Butch's abuse. She may have felt that the abuse was escalating or had gotten to a very dangerous level. She also may have just snapped because she was unable to handle all the abuse and pressure in the marriage. It also may have been because Mrs. Maggie felt that Mama was not old enough, or responsible enough to keep and care for the boys as she should have. We don't know anything, for certain since we never really talked to her about it. It is only speculation and Otis was the only one there and he was too young to know what happened.

Mama was told later that Mrs. Maggie took the boys to Elkhart, Texas where they stayed with relatives for while. In any case Mama didn't see them until many years later. Their rearing was taken over by Rev. Will and Mrs. Maggie. Their father was supposed to be there in the house with them when he was home, as well. Even though he was in the home, Otis remembers that time as being very rugged. They were without so many of the things that one needs to make life easier.

It is so odd to me that they lived all their young lives in the same community as Mama and the rest of us, their brothers and sisters! We didn't see each other or have any contact until much later. They even went to school at the same school where my older brothers and sisters went to, and where I started. I found that amazing.

They lived in the community near Shiloh Baptist church where the rest of their family belonged. They even had some of the same teachers we all had. It seems strange that some of us, the younger ones including me, did not know about it!

Otis, my oldest brother says he was a teenager (about 13) when he saw his Mama again! Yet, he and Cotis knew and were friends with so many of the same people that we knew and were friends with, even our closest neighbors!

At the time Otis saw her again, Mama had remarried and had other children. We began visiting with them whenever Daddy and Mama could. I can remember some of those visits with them at their grandmother's home. We went in Daddy's old Model A/T truck. I don't know what kind of truck it really was, but that it wasn't a top of the line vehicle. It was one that daddy only drove as far as the grocery store because half the time it had no licenses plates. These visits continued for years. After that time our brothers started coming to visit us.

Being a mother myself, I believe this was the time when Mama's walk with God became so powerful and diligent. The time when Mama came to the realization that God would always be there. Knowing what a mother feels for a child and how much she would have missed them, I know that it was only with God's strength that she was able to stay sane in a time like that.

"**The Lord will provide**" became her mantra, one that Mama quoted often, when things looked bleak. She also had a song on her lips most of the times when she was alone or just busy. One could tell by the tenor of the song if she were happy, sad or worried. There was a gospel song or hymn that she would think of and sing to fit whatever the situation.

Otis went to the army when he came of age and Cotis went to Dallas soon after. When Otis was discharged he went to Dallas, too.

Upon getting away from Mr. Butch, Mama lived with Mrs. Georgia Ann Williams, in the Shiloh Community not too far from the Shiloh Baptist Church.

Family, That's Us

To God the family was His greatest most cherished creation.
He used His own hands to form it, with thought and concentration.
He made man alone at first, after speaking into being all he would need on earth
From man's side He created woman, a helpmeet, with this action to family He gave birth.
*In Biblical times all who were by the **father** were counted as the household*
*We've become more up-to-date; now, we include **mothers** in this unified family fold.*
So we go back as far as we can in finding out about our family tree
Just not Daddy's folks, but also Mama's early ancestry
You see there are folks that can lay claim to you no matter who they or you are
Even though you might wish they'd claim someone away from you extremely far
They are that group of people that share a special something with you
That identifies them in ways that identifies you, too.
You know, the kind of things; genes, a name, a home, a face
A personal relative, a habit or a growing up place
It might be an illness, a secret fault even the same grade in school
A special quirk and kink in your gene pool
Whatever it is, you can't readily deny
All you can do is carry on and ask, "Lord why?"
Some are persons you long to visit and stay with for a little or long while
Who may want to know, or already know what you were like as a child

Those souls you present or introduce to others
As parents, grandparents, aunts, uncles, cousins, sisters and brothers
The folks you want to love and stand by you through thick and thin
And whose approval of you, you always expect to win
Yes they are the roots, trunk, limbs, and leaves on your personal small or large tree
Because they go to make up your natural family!

Daddy

2nd Husband Will Dexter Jones

"Mr. Will"

There are two people who are so important in the life of a child
Those persons that just hearing their names may cause one nostalgia or smile
One of them is that of a very loving mother
The second is usually of her partner; your dad is the name of other.

~~~~~~

We have come to the part of this discourse where my daddy's family history, gets our attention. Wig and Middie Freeman were a couple who had four girls whose names were; Lula, Maxie, Cora and Aida.

One daughter, Lula Freeman met and married Clemmon Jones. Their marriage produced Lean, Laura, Georgia and Will Dexter, born on August 10, 1888 (my daddy) while they were a couple. (I have no idea where they called home.)

Grandpa Clemmon passed away, and Lula met and married a man named Price Cox. Part of their married life was lived in Wortham, Texas. This union gave Daddy more siblings; P. C. (May 18, 1896), Edward and Amy Cox. The two brothers somewhere along the way moved to Hugo, Oklahoma to live and his youngest sister Amy went to live in Dallas.

The paternal side of Daddy's family, Grandpa Clemons's mother and dad was not available to this recorder. I have no idea where Daddy and his older sisters were reared. What I do know, was that somewhere along the line he began living in the Shiloh community.

Daddy's first marriage was to a lady named Darcus Wade. The products of Mrs. Darcus' and Daddy's marriage were two daughters. The first, Cardelia who was older than Mama, born August, 1908 or 1909 and the second daughter, Lula Mae, born January 8, 1911, who was just 6 months younger than Mama!

Mrs. Darcus, their mother died. However, he had another daughter somewhere along the way, her name was Edith, but we all referred to her as Edie. She was the daughter of Darcus' sister, Rosie Wade, *his sister-in-law*, who was raised by him!

Later, Daddy married his second wife Mrs. Teasey. Their marriage I am told did not last very long. Yet, while they were together they purchased property in the Butler/Shiloh community. It was a small farm of a little more than 123 acres, with only a fraction less than half of which was covered with trees, and still is.

The land they purchased was done on the 15th of January, 1923 at 2:00 P.M. in the afternoon! (I know all this because, I obtained the original records. It was on that deed to the property they bought back then.) The deed included another document with the signature of the long ago Texas governor, **Elisha Pease** on it. It was written on some old rice-skin paper he signed back on February 25, **1854** to a grant for this land, in Austin, Texas!

On the property was a small house that was to be our home until after Daddy passed away and where nine of my siblings and I were born. This was the property that he and Aunt Georgia lived on, as well as his daughter, Lula, and her family for some time.

The marriage of Daddy and Mrs. Teasey went south. I can't say it was before or after, a love relationship developed between Daddy and Mama. But, I do firmly believe Mama's and Daddy's was a real love match (Of course I would, they were **my** mother and dad!). The evidence was there in the way they were around each other, and the way they looked at each other. They had a special something you could even feel.

Daddy and Mrs. Teasey were separated in 1934, and she signed over her rights to any of the property. The land had not been paid for since it was only a few years after they purchased it. He continued paying on it until his death, Mama then paid off the balance after his death.

Mama was staying with Georgia Ann Jones Williams, Daddy's sister. That meant she was on a section of land that was purchased by Daddy, and his second wife Teasey. So when he trapped, hunted and fished on the property He passed by. Mama said she first saw Daddy as he was going back and forth to check on his traps that were in the pasture near Aunt Georgia's house.

Will Jones, Daddy, was a much older man, than Mama. He was born in 1888, meaning that since she was born on May 3, 1910, he was about twenty two years older than Mama.
He also had those two marriages under his belt. Even at that time that was probably a bit unique. This comment comes because of his past history.

When she met him, she must have started calling him 'Mr. Will.' The name stuck. As far as she was concerned that was his name. She never referred to him as anything other than 'Mr. Will' as long I knew her!

Daddy was a person who loved to laugh. He was also one for telling stories and jokes that would make other folk laugh, too. In spite of his being much older we never noticed the age difference because of his lively attitude and the fact that she always seemed happy.

Daddy was able to hold on to the property even when other black land owners in our area lost theirs. He allowed no one else to have/keep the original deed to the land. He was told it would be better if he did allow someone in a more solid position to keep it on several occasions, by a few prominent men in the area. I was within hearing distance when the last man tried to get him to, "Let me hold that old deed of yours, safely for you!"I think were the words he used.

My daddy's reply would not look so nice in print even if I could spell it all, or even repeated orally. But, I am sure he got the message across that time. No one else came to him to make that suggestion again. Nor to any of us, that maybe they would be better able to safely keep up with his deed and other papers!

By the time of his marriage to Mama, Daddy's two older daughters had married.

 Cardelia, had married to Jesse Willis and Lula Mae, was married to Tracy Willis, his brother. They both had children of their own by then, too. That means Daddy's children by Mama have nieces and nephews a lot older than they are.

Edie was also married. Her husband was John Brown. Her oldest child, a son (Ausie) born before her marriage been given to Daddy.

When Mama and Daddy married, Edie's son Ausie came to live with them. (He was later to be officially adopted by them.)

Mama's and Daddy's marriage was also very fruitful, since they became parents of Elouise (December 10,), their oldest daughter, their oldest biological son Carlton Calvin (August 11,), Willie Clemmons (April 19,)

Evelyn Juanita (December 2,) Eddie Marie (February 13, **that's me.),** Isaiah (December 18,) Laura Lee (January 10,) Georgia Mae (February 7,) Venus Lean March 13,) and then there was Marvin born in1946, (who passed away within a week or so after birth).

We lived in Daddy's small unpainted house. It had "almost" four rooms. It was the house that was on the property when he and Mrs. Teasey had purchased it. It was small unpainted structure with boards that straight up and down rather than across as most houses today. It had only about three windows of regular size and the one in the kitchen.

When looking at the house, what you would have seen was a dark grayish structure with a wooden shingled roof. To get an up close and personal tour we will start at the back of the house. Coming toward the back door one had to pass the wood pile, on the left side and the well, where we got all our water on the right.

'The **well'** was a hole in the ground with a top made of a square wooden frame built around it, that had a bucket tied to a rope that was held up and let down by a pulley that would let the bucket down into the hole where the water was.

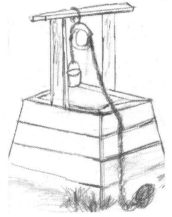

A crude replica of '**The well'**

This would allow the bucket to fill up, and one could then pull it back up, pour the water into whatever containers that were available.

The location of the well was just a few steps from the back door. This made it more convenient for getting water into the house when it was needed. There was a small storage house that we called 'the smokehouse,' because it held the salt-cured meat of animals killed for food on the farm, at the right as you were going inside. It also held a few other things that there was no room for, in the house. A few steps from the smokehouse you got to the back door to the kitchen.

Upon entering the kitchen door, you saw an old wood stove in one corner to the left along the wall facing you, with a storage part at the top. The stove top had a smooth area where the cooking was done, but there was a bit of sooty black in places that even when cleaned often, only stayed clean for a short while. In back of the stove was the woodpile with wood for the stove. There was what we called a 'safe' a storage container not large enough to be called a pantry, but was where the utensils and the dry foods were kept on the wall opposite the stove. There was an old icebox along the wall to the left, under the small window, that when, it had a block of ice in it, we were able to use as a refrigerator.

Beside the back door where you came in on the left was the very important *washstand*. It held the water buckets, which most of the times were filled with water to be used in the house, unless it was near time for the refilling of them. On the front part of the stand was the 'wash pan' a small enameled bowl used like a face bowl.

Above the stand on the wall was a nail that held *the* towel. This towel was used by **everybody** who washed up there. It was what everyone used to dry their faces and hands on after washing up there. The very same towel! (It left me with the very strong desire for a towel I had to use only **one** time! That wish has stayed with me. The **first** things I think of giving as wedding gifts, even today, is a set of towels!)

Across from the stove and other stuff that was the in the kitchen, was the bed in which my brothers slept. It was only what one could call a half-room. It was off to the other side of the kitchen. It was not really separated from the kitchen because there was no wall between the table where we ate and the bed where the boys slept. There was a beam across the ceiling where one could hang a quilt, sheet, or large piece of cloth to give the boys a bit of privacy when necessary.

Going through the door to the next room you passed near the table where we sat as a family to eat. The door you went through was across from the back door. Passing through it one entered a bedroom-sitting/family room. In other words, it was the main room of the house. This was the front room of the house if one came from the front yard, it was where the wood heater was, (the only source of heat in the winter except for the kitchen stove, for the whole house). This room had extra wood chairs for regular family and company. This was also the room where Mama and Daddy slept.

In it there was also a dresser, bed and a homemade bench. The only other furniture in the room was a tin and wood traveling trunk used as a combination closet, wardrobe, a storage trunk and, at times an extra seat.

This was also the room where we had Family Prayer **every** Sunday morning. It was also what we would call today the family room. The Family Prayer Time, included singing, scripture, prayer/s and recited bible verses. **It was not delayed or skipped at any time!**

I can remember sometimes we wished it had been maybe, skipped or done later. This was during the times when some of us had young people, visiting with us. We were not always sure how our visiting friends would react to the activity, especially when they were expected to be able to recite a Bible verse during the Prayer Time. This was always done just before breakfast was to be served on Sunday morning.

We had one memorable Sunday morning during Family Prayer Time, when a couple of Ausie and Carlton's friends were visiting. It came after Mama and Daddy read the scripture and prayed. This was the time for all of us to give a Bible verse. Everyone was saying their verses and it came time for them to recite theirs. One of them mumbled, "***Throw a rock in the church!***"

After his comment, one could have heard a pin drop! We were completely speechless or in shock, for a few long seconds. All of us, the children, were wondering, what in the world our parents would say?

Then Daddy, with his odd sense of humor, burst out laughing. Still smiling, Daddy told him, "Son, I think you need to read your parents' Bible a little."

Mama hid a smile by holding the Bible in front of her face. We were both surprised and relieved that neither one of them got angry nor reprimanded the young man. He, their friend, was quite embarrassed. Many of us still remember the incident, though it was to say the least, sometime ago. (It has been over 60 years ago!)

At our house our parents expected all of us to know Bible verses. This was part of our home training. We were required to attend church **every** Sunday unless we were too sick to do so. That included Sunday school, Baptist Young Peoples Union (BYPU), and church services on the Sunday they had it. We had only had church on two Sundays a month, because our pastor was an itinerant one. If one didn't feel up to going to church on Sunday, one was out of everything that went on that day, too! You couldn't suddenly feel all right after church was over.

Now let's get back to the house we lived, and were born in. Leading from Mama and Daddy's room was a door to the next room where all of us girls slept. It was also used as the living room, where extra chairs were set up for my older sister, when she entertained her boyfriends/had a date with them. There were chairs set up near the window. There were two iron double beds in the room also. All of the older girls slept there altogether. To make more room, two of us slept with our heads toward the head of the bed, and one with her head toward the foot of the bed or vice versa. This was the whole house.

I am sure one reading this would be wondering since I have described all I could remember, about the old house, I did not include a **bathroom**. Well, I didn't include the description of one because there was no bathroom in the house!

We washed up in the kitchen and bathed in a #3 tin washtub. Bathing didn't occur as often during the week as one does today. You had to go to the well outside and get the water, put it on the wood stove, get the fire started to warm the water, pour it in the tub with enough cool water to make it just right then for bathing. You also had to find a room where everyone was somewhere else at the time so you could be alone made the experience special. It probably occurred about once a week. Only at special times did it occur a little more often. For our 'regular **business**' one went outside. If it was night or one was sick there was an enameled bucket with a top that we called the "slop jar" that was there for that purpose.

THE LOOK OF THE ORIGINAL HOME PLACE

Mama, and all of us children, helped to make a living on the farm, where we helped to grow crops of corn, peas, cotton, watermelon, peanuts, maize, and sugar cane to name a few. We were also into the rearing a few cows, hogs, horses, mules and poultry; such as chickens, turkeys and even guineas. These were the farming activities of the people around us as well. Some of the animals were there to be of assistance to our effort as farmers and some to help supply us with another needed source of food.

Mama was quite friendly with all the people in the community, though I feel she thought of Mrs. Metta Malone as her best and closest friend. She was one of our closest neighbors. Mrs. Metta and Mr. Sterling Malone lived right across the field from us. With her she shared many visits and I imagine confidences as well. They participated in many other activities together. I think she felt she could count on Mrs. Metta even in times she felt distanced from the other folks in the community.

Mr. Sam and Mrs. Stacia Cornish lived across the creek form the Malones. They were close to us as well. Even though they were not related to us, that we know of, we called her Cousin Stacia and her daughters called Mama Cousin Babe, as did so many other people in the community.

Mama may have been very young when she came into the area, but she developed close relationships with all the folks there. Lula, Daddy's second daughter and her family even lived on part of the property for awhile until they bought other property and moved about a mile or so away across the woods. We visited all of them as family and neighbors frequently. We also helped each other out during our farming chores.

Edie lived in Plum Creek and Cardelia in an area up near Dallas. We saw and visited with Lula and her family quite regularly. Her children attended school and church with us as well. We a spent many nights at each other's houses.

All the children, Cardelia's, Lula's and Edie's, called Mama, **Cousin** Babe! Since our sisters were so much older than we were, we had called all three sisters Aunties! They were Aunt Cardelia, Aunt Lula, and Aunt Edie to each of us for most of our lives. Some of us still refer to them that way.

Many were the times we all, had to go on long trips to West Texas to work crops as itinerant workers. We would chop and pick cotton, harvest onions, maize and corn. Many times we all had to register for school a few weeks after school started because we were away working so we could have enough money to make it the next few months.

We worked away in places like Midland, Lubbock, Palmer, Ferris, Corsicana, Ennis, and Vernon, of Will Bogger County as well as other areas that produced crops where they needed hands to either, help plant, tend or harvest. When we went on one of those itinerant farm workers trips we would pack up the essential things we would need and ride in the backs of Daddy's old truck. At other times the hiring entity would send a truck or, drive the truck himself that was to take us to the work site. We would travel for hours and sometimes all night and day, depending on how long it took to reach the place needing workers.

Once we arrived there we had to stay in some very poorly, hastily built or put together shanties-houses. They had no beds so we all had to sleep on the floor on mattresses we had brought from home for that purpose. These houses had nothing most of the times except a wood stove for cooking, if that. Sometimes they didn't even have that, and cooking was done outdoors over an open fire. None of them had any bathrooms, so we had to use outhouses, or 'the bushes' the way we referred to the places we would hide to use the restroom.

It was on one of these trips that I had the experience of being in sandstorms! They were not activities I'd wish to repeat and would not recommend for anyone else either. We were in the area once known as part of the "Dustbowl." It was on one or these trips that I also got to see, and spend time with my mother's older sister Lellure Jennings, her husband Uncle George Washington Jennings and family. They lived in the area of Vernon, Texas in Will Bogger County. We had never had the chance to get to know her or meet our cousins before that time.

George Washington Jennings

Lellure Jennings

Ewatha Jennings

We were surprised to know that one of my cousins, Ewatha, had been struck by lightning and survived! I always thought she was so cute. In fact so was her sister Cherry.

We enjoyed this trip even though we were supposed to just be working *because* we got to visit with family. Visiting with this family was something we didn't get to do very much unless they were in the same community and/or not very far away.

Not many of Mama's or Daddy's relatives were around during our growing up, except Aunt Georgia. They had all moved out of the area to places that were not close to where we lived. There was only about a couple times, that I can remember, spending time with Daddy's brothers because they were residents of Hugo, Oklahoma. We didn't get to really know any of his family except Aunt Georgia. As stated before, she lived up the road from us. His two older sisters, Aunt Lean and Laura had passed away before I came along. His youngest sister Amy lived in Dallas, Texas. His brother's trips to our house were brief.

Uncle P. C. and Uncle Ed (Edward) Cox visited those few times to see Daddy and us. On those times because they came together, it was just the two them. We didn't get to meet their families. Their trips were from so far away they didn't bring their families. Even with all the tremendous improvement of cars and roads today this trip is still a distance of a day, by car, from our home.

Back then, it would have taken much longer, and especially since cars were so much smaller they wouldn't carry very many people. We were unable to go there to see them, until we were grown. By then Daddy and, his brothers were gone. (Daddy may have visited them alone, while he did those working tours for the railroad companies when he needed the money. Those trips sometimes took him all the way to Kansas and he would pass through Oklahoma.)

During the rare times our uncles did come, it turned into an enjoyably large gathering of family. On those occasions we got visits from my older sisters; Cardelia, and her family, Lula and her family, Aunt Georgia and sometimes Edie and her family all joined us at the house. It was good that each time, If I remember correctly, they came it was during fair weather. I have no idea what it would have been like with all of us inside our small house. At these gatherings we had lots of food that Mama, Aunt Georgia and Lula put together.

Aunt Amy, Daddy's younger sister, came a bit more often since she lived closer. We got to meet her daughter Cleo. (Her other children I didn't get know. My sister Elouise and other members of the family got to know her better when they all moved to the Dallas area after they left home, before she passed away.)

The memories of my father and mother together are what lead me to believe they were a real love match. Although they didn't do the 'lovey-dovey' thing around us, they seemed always to be so comfortable with each other. Daddy's love or laughter was usually more active when she was there.

He also loved telling stories and jokes that would make others laugh too. That part of his personality is what readily comes to mind when I think of him, the way he laughed, and how very loud his laugher was. Mama was of a quiet nature. She would display her smile often, but she was not one to do the kind of belly laughs Daddy liked to do.

Since I have been married I have realized that Mama was more like what the Bible says a wife is supposed to be. In spite of his happy demeanor most of the times, Daddy would sometimes display a very volatile temper. He could say some words when he was agitated that you would not even **want** to ever find even, in a dictionary since you knew already they were not nice. Mama's reaction to his temper, most of the time, was just ignore him and what was going on. Not a victim in any way, she would just smile at him or, start humming a little tune. Mama most of the times would not say anything hostile, in fact, she didn't say anything at all. Daddy would usually just do his ranting and raving, then throw up his hands and leave the scene.

In other words she had a kind of calming force in him, except for one particular time.

This was the one time when Daddy's temper seemed to get to the point where, all of us, and, other members of the family really got bothered. This time all the family near us got involved!

Daddy spoke really long and loudly to/or at Mama one day. His activity was so alarming that one of my brothers, I think it was Carlton, ran to our older sister Lula's house. After hearing what he had to say, she and her husband come over. Aunt Georgia came too, my brother told her as he passed her house going to Sister Lula's, but she heard the ruckus from her house, anyway, Daddy was so that loud!

When she got there, my Sister Lula asked Mama if she wanted to leave. She didn't really answer her. She just sat, rocking in the rocking chair.

All of the children, who were still at home, were in the yard talking to each other about what was going on, and wondering what in the world was going on, and what it had all started about.

I also know it was the only time that there was a serious disagreement in the family between Daddy and Mama. And I do mean it was *serious.* Even then, Mama kept her cool and took very little part in the uproar. She just sat in the rocking chair humming. She talked to those who talked to her, except Daddy, while he was yelling.

The disturbance lasted for some time but it was finally over. When it was over Mama cooked for all of us and the visitors that were there! Daddy was back to his old self by then, talking and laughing out loud. To this day I don't have any idea what the ruckus started about. I just know it ended with a family gathering that was similar to many others. Mama and none of us went anywhere we just sat and ate!

Yes, one could see that in spite of Daddy having a usually happy demeanor most of the times, he was one for being quite volatile at others. When something went wrong or he was angry he could also say some words that one did not want to say or find in any dictionary. They didn't usually even print those kinds of words anywhere in those days!

As a good example, there was another memorable time I can remember his using of words that was unacceptable, was a time when one of the mules had upset him out in the pasture. He had a single tree in his hand. A single-tree was a tool used so that a single mule or horse could pull a plow, wagon or sled.

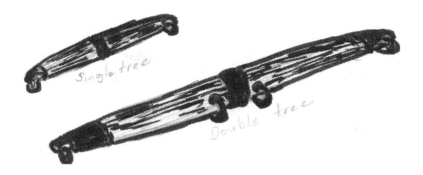

Some of us, kids, were in the yard at the house but we could hear him yelling at the mules all way out in the pasture. All of a sudden he took the single tree and threw it down the slope and hit the barn! That was a real good distance away.

His voice was so loud that Mama could hear him in the kitchen, and his language was such that Mama was disturbed. She came out, put her hands on her hips and called up to him.

"Mr. Will, Mr. Will! Did you know that me, **and** the children can hear you all the way down here? Is that the kind of language you want them to use?"

Daddy burst out laughing and called back, "Hell, no. Tell them to cover up their damn ears! That old mule, Slim, is being a real so and so!" (Only so-n-so was not the word he used)

Even though Daddy seemed aggravated, there was a smile on his face while he was yelling back at Mama.

"You need to clean up your language!" She said and threw up her hands waving as she went back into the kitchen.

This was one of the few times I don't remember seeing his pipe in his mouth. He was a pipe smoker and his pipe seemed to have been an integral part of his face. It was so much of a part of his mouth he had a worn an indentation into his teeth to fit the shape of the pipe's handle.

I can remember on more than a few occasions when he had almost everyone in the house looking for his pipe. He would yell, "Where is my pipe?"

When we all heard that yell we'd start looking no matter where we were, then there were the times Mama would come into the room where he was, take one look at Daddy and say, "Mr. Will, "What is that the thing you have in your mouth that you keeping puffing on?"

"Oh, I guess that's my pipe," he'd say with a grin, and probably say something else like, "I had ya'll going there for a moment didn't I?"

In spite of his volatile temper, he was the kind of father we could sit on his lap and braid the long bangs he wore across the front of his head and combed to the back of his head that he always had cut short. We usually did it during the times were together as a family, in the evenings, in their room.

During breakfast in the mornings he would also give us a sip of his coffee, when Mama wasn't looking. He'd put more milk in the saucer than coffee, and tell us not to let Mama see him give it to us. She would pretend not to notice, but she knew all along.

One time I remember going to pick berries Mama, Evelyn and Mrs. Metta and her daughter, Frances. We went off to ourselves to pick. We were eating as many berries as we could and kept talking; at least Evelyn and Frances were.

Frances asked, "Did you see Lou Willie at church last Sunday? She spent the whole time we were in the choir..."

I heard a disturbing sound in the bushes where we were picking and I screeched. "Evelyn! Francis! Did ya'll hear that?" I yelled.

When they quieted down they heard it too. "I think..... Oh my! It's a snake! Francis yelled and she and Evelyn took off running, dropping the berries as they ran.

I stood there as the snake came into sight. It seemed like the biggest, longest one in the world! Suddenly I heard someone screaming their lungs out as I passed out completely.

When I came to Mama, Mrs. Metta, the other girls and the dogs were standing over me. Mama was bathing my face with a damp cloth. She looked really worried. I opened my eyes yelling 'Mama, I saw the biggest snake! He was coming at me. I thought it was going to bite and kill me! Did he? Did he bite me? Am I hurt, Mama?"

"No dear, I don't think he had a chance to bite you. We were able to kill him before he got completely out of the vines after you screamed so loud. You know you gave us all quite a scare."

When we returned home that evening, Evelyn and I didn't let anybody talk about much of anything else.

The rest of the summer the rest of the summer seemed to go by slowly, then it was September and time for school again, only I wasn't old enough yet. The first morning Elouise, Carlton, Evelyn, and Willie C. got all dressed up early. Mama fixed breakfast. We all ate together then they left for school.

Mama gave her usual directions that they be good. I stood in the yard and spoke to our neighbors, Frances, Dutch, Lovie, Ruby Faye, Sarah and Mable Cornish as they all had to pass our house on the way to school.

After school one day Evelyn and Frances came to the house with a girl I didn't know. She told Mama her name was Theresa Isadore. After staring at her every chance I got for what seemed like ages I got up enough courage to ask her, "Why are your hands so rough and scared?"

She was a nice looking girl, but her hands were in horrible condition. Where the hands are usually has dark marks, and creases that are a bit darker than the other part, they were eaten away into deep crevices, and the rest was really very rough looking. Her hands were rough both inside and out and the skin color was very dark.

"Well they got that way when I had to wash some things with pure lye." She told me.

She talked so nicely with everyone. She also told us a bit about herself. She said she had lost her mother several months before and she lived with her father and he traveled frequently from one place to another. They had just moved into our community.

For some reason she ended up spending the night with us. After she and the rest of my siblings had gone to school Mama dressed the baby (Laura) and, Zip and I had put on our clothes. While she combed my hair she told me my panties were hanging on the line outside and they were just about dry. She told me to go out to the line and get them when she finished my hair and put them on.

Daddy was going out to the church and she told me I could go with him and, that I could go by the school while he was next door at the church. I was in such a state of excitement I forgot to put my panties on! I ran and danced around Daddy all the way there. Daddy went on to the church and I ran to the school. When I got there Evelyn and Theresa were outside for recess.

I ran up to them. "Evelyn, Theresa! Mama let me come to the school for a little while!"

Theresa came over and swung me up causing the air to circulate under my dress making me acutely aware that I had nothing under my dress and slip. So I scream "Let me down! Let me down! Please!" I was trying desperately to get my hands on the bottom of my dress.

She thought I was just scared and said "Oh don't be afraid, I'm not going to hurt you!" She started to whirl me around. By that time we had an audience and when she started to put me down my dress went out a bit. It was just enough for some of those watching to realize that I was minus my underwear!

Evelyn came rushing up to us. She asked very angrily, "Eddie, where in the world are your panties? Don't you know that you don't go around without underwear on?"

I felt so embarrassed I just couldn't hold back the tears. "I forgot them, Mama told they were on the fence but I was so glad to be on the way here I didn't realize that I didn't stop to put them on."

"Go over to the church and tell Daddy you have to go back home put some on. You can come back if it's alright with him and Mama." She told me.

I told Evelyn bitterly, "I don't want to come back to this old school! Can't you see everybody here is laughing at me!"

"What did you expect, coming out here like that?"

When I got home and Mama found out what had happened and I told her I didn't want to go to school. She patted my cheek and told me, "There are things we go through that we cause ourselves. Sometimes we just have to ask the Lord to help us get though them. You are in that place now. But you need not hate school it won't always be like that."

As the years have gone by I think of that time with a bit of a flinch, wondering how I could have forgotten my underwear.

The next year I began school, but I only spent about one year at Shiloh, then I went to Owens Chapel elementary. Even though some of the same children were there, there were others and no one even mentioned my mishap.

Mama had another child, another little girl, Georgia, increasing our immediate family to nine including Ausie, who was still away in the war. Lula one of my father's three older daughters, lived in the community and had children that attended the same school.

Mama's two older sons were living with their grandmother, in the same community, and by this time we were visiting them every once in a while.

Lula's children were more like our cousins than our nieces and nephews. Especially since many of them were so much older than we were. Mama treated them like they were just part of the family, maybe nieces and nephews.

When I got to third grade I had some experiences that remain with me even until today. Some of my schoolmates who were in the same room with me, (each room had about three grades in the same room) seem always to always find some way to make me feel a little like a freak because of the clothes I wore, the way my hair was or something else since I became avid reader, I believe, I had learned to read. So, I didn't always keep up with what was going on around me because I had my head in a book.

Because of my talks with Mama about what other folk would do if you were slightly different for whatever reason. I had gotten to a point where I had developed kind of a resistance to a lot of the comments made about me. But one day I had problems from some of them from the start of the day.

That morning as I came into the building with my books, one of the girls who had been regularly doing things she thought would irritate me, laughed and said loudly, "Oh look Eddie has a new coat. It was given to her by Mrs. Catherine. Wasn't it nice of her husband to give it to her?"

She knew we had received a bunch of clothes from the family because she had been at the store when Mr. Mimn told Daddy to come by the house they had some things. She had already seen me on the bus and knew that I had been wearing a coat that was quite worn before.

I really liked the coat and was so glad to have it. I smiled and patted the coat as I kept saying to myself inside, "Mama says people who laugh at other folks, are to be pitied. They feel like they are lacking something or they wouldn't have to try and put someone else down."
I kept repeating this to myself to hold back the remarks I know would probably have gotten me in trouble.

Besides, I said something else to myself, "I am warm and have a coat on that I really like! Why should I care what they think?"

I went on the outside and waited until the bell sounded. I liked school because I had a good time even during classes. I usually made very good grades. I also thought the teachers liked me because of it. Later during recess Nell, the girl who had made the sarcastic remarks, came up to me bringing a bunch of other girls and a few boys.

She said, pretending to sound sweet, "Eddie, are you very hungry?"

I pretended I didn't hear her. I was standing under a tree near the edge of the school yard watching some more students on the swings, and some others were playing hopscotch. I was waiting for someone to stop and allow me a turn on the swing when she finished.

While I thought no one else was looking I had seen a cookie on the ground. It looked so good, I was hungry. Breakfast had been a long time ago, I picked it up and was almost finished eating it when they came up. I was not planning on answering her.

But, she continued her little speech, "Eddie, if I had known you were so hungry you'd pick up dirty cookies off the ground I'd have given some of my lunch. Wouldn't I, Sarah?" talking to one of the girls there.

In the same fake sweet voice, "I sure would have if I had known."

As she finished she and the other kids burst into giggles.

Then Nell said, with false sweetness, "The poor thing. She must not have gotten her hair combed today. I wonder if her mother was so busy with all those other children she has."

By this time the group had grown. They had made almost a complete circle around me. Nell seemed to appreciate having this audience to listen to her. She got even louder. "Honey why did you mama plait your hair that way? Isn't that rather odd?"

I had taken all I thought I could. I knew Mama had tried to teach me to turn the other cheek or not to say anything if it was not nice, but I felt this time she'd feel I had a right to stop her or I didn't think at all.

I lit into her with a vengeance! With both hands and feet!

My actions were so unexpected because I had never done anything like it before. She was caught off guard, so were the other children. Later I heard one of the kids talking, "She clobbered Nell in nothing flat! Nobody knew she was that mad. "

After the skirmish was over the children moved off to their own little groups. I straightened up and silently hoped that no one told Mama about what happened.

In a few minutes the bell sounded and we all went back into the classroom. Oddly enough no one told the teacher! It seemed as if we all had signed a truce of silence.

Later on that day, the teacher told the third graders to put their heads on our tables and rest for a while. It was warm in the room so I dropped off to sleep. When I woke up my teacher was standing over me glaring.

"Wake up, Eddie! Where do you think you are?

I sat up and rubbed my eyes as I said, "I'm sorry Ma'am; I didn't mean to go to sleep."

She went back to the front of the room and started a discussion with the fourth graders and I began with the writing assignment she had placed on the blackboard. A boy named James was sitting across the table from me. He bent down under the table and began to pull at the leather on my shoe that had worn loose from my shoe. I kicked at him and told him.

"Leave me alone, will you?"

Nell's cousin was sitting just down the table from me and looked up at that time only to turn her head in such a way as to let me know she was not my friend. But, I went back to my work. After a few more minutes of work I got up, asked the teacher if I could be excused to go to the restroom. She gave me permission.

I went to the restroom on the back side of the campus. I was ready to go back inside when Nell's cousins came toward me and looked at me real funny and smiled as I passed her. When I got back into the room the teacher was looking as if she was ready to explode.

"Eddie Jones. Get up here!"

I was puzzled because I had no idea what was going on.

When I got to her desk she yelled, "Have lost your mind? Did you just ask James to go to the restroom with you?"

There were a lot of smothered snickers around the room. I was so shocked I couldn't answer.

She continued, "Well, don't you have anything to say?"

I stood there gaping still puzzled unable to say anything. But, I got my gumption back after a minute, fisted my hand by my side and told her, "Ma'am, I didn't say anything to James except to ask him to leave my shoes alone!"

Nell popped up at the back of the room and said, "Yes, she did, I heard her. Some of the others did too." She turned to her friends and asked, "Didn't you?"

Almost all of them either nodded heads or mumbled accent.

James seemed just as puzzled as I was. He finally said angrily. "Nell, you didn't hear nobody say anything! You're just mad!"

Nell said angrily, "I did too, hear her, and so did the others girls!"

The teacher looked at me disgustedly, and then proceeded to give one of the longest lectures I had ever heard from her before. I had the feeling of being denigrated in front of everybody.

I was crying heartbrokenly by the end of her lecture. I was so disappointed that she didn't believe me or James. She would not even listen to either one of us. She even decided to whip me just because of what Nell had said!

The rest of the day was the worst I had spent in my life. The other kids heckled me and the teacher seemed to be overly strict and hard with me for the rest of the day. After that school wasn't such a nice place for the rest of that school year.

Mama and Daddy knew about the incident and believed me but they were the kind of parents who felt that their interference would only make matters worse. They just told me to trust in the Lord to take care of me. Despite my letdowns, I made it through the year. Then I got my report card and realized I had been retained in third grade for another year!

I was so shocked because felt that I had been a good student. I had always been good in reading; I could repeat most of the stories in the book, arithmetic, in spelling because I had helped my older sister who was older than me with hers and the other subjects too. I had always gotten good grades on my other report cards. I was not only hurt I was confused. I was still crying about it when I got home.

My parents were confused as well. They had not gone to the school before, but this time they went to the school the next day.

Their question was why, since I had been making good grades all school year I was retained? They knew I had studied something until I knew most of it by memory. Reading had always been my favorite subject. I could even repeat most of the stories in the book by memory.

The answer they got was that I had missed too many days during the year.

Mama told me when they got back. Then we talked about what had happened the year before and remembered that during the cotton picking season we were away for some time. We had gone to pick cotton in west Texas and my father had fallen ill out in the field. He was taken to hospital where he remained for about three weeks. When he came back to the camp house we had to tend him in bed for a good while. Someone also had to take him back every three days for shots.

"Honey, you must also remember, that, with all the extra bills for Daddy's illness we had to stay a bit longer than intended. You were all out of school at least two weeks longer than expected. On top of that, Eddie, you have been sick on a few other occasions that kept you here. Remember you had no coat and had missed more days for that too. So there is nothing we can do honey."

We all knew Daddy would whip us when we misbehaved yet, it somehow didn't prevent those time we got ourselves onto situations where a punishment was warranted. He didn't usually whip any one of us if he was really mad. Yet, there were times when that didn't hold true. It would be those times when he would say something like, "Well young squirt," you knew then you were not just in trouble, but **BIG** trouble. You were about to really get it!

My brother Willie C. tells me about the time Daddy and the older children were hoeing in the field right next to Aunt Georgia's house when Daddy asked our brother, Carlton to go to the well and bring back a bucket of water.

Where they were working, they could see the well from the field. Carlton walked slowly to the well. When he got to the well he put the bucket down into the well then, lazily pulled it up as he would lie down on the ground. He would do this at each pull, until the bucket came completely up, then he slowly got up and poured the water into the bucket. He then he walked along with the bucket keeping the same pace he had while drawing the water. Slow.

In the meantime Daddy had been watching his activity from the field. He went and broke off a switch and laid it next one of the posts of the closest fence. He then went back and continued working in the field as Carlton got near the place where the switch was. He called out, "Carlton, bring me that 'hurry up medicine' over there by that post!"

Carlton picked up the switch and carried it over to him. It had not dawned on him that he was the one who was about to get it, until Daddy said, "Young squirt', do you think it should take all day to bring us a bucket of water up here?"

Carlton realized then that he was in for it. He then made another very bad decision. Maybe, he thought because Daddy was old and had on laced up high-topped boots he could out run him. He ran.

Daddy took off after him everyone, especially Carlton, was surprised that Daddy caught up with him, and so quickly. This was one time Daddy really seemed mad. He would usually hit a person about three or four times and quit, but this time Carlton got quite a bit more. He got enough hits that Aunt Georgia came out into her yard and yelled at Daddy.

"Buddy, you've given him enough already!" It wasn't until then that he stopped.

I don't remember Willie c saying they drank the water.

Mama usually meted out the physical punishments most of the times. Her whippings were not nearly as severe but, they were just as dreaded. She didn't just spank one of us; she gave us a whole *sermon* to go along with it. You never got one without it. You knew why, you being punished and, everything she could think of, that could have resulted badly from what you had done.

Carlton wasn't the only one Daddy got real good. We all got some kind of punishment when we misbehaved badly enough for him to mete out the punishment. They just were not quite of the nature as the one that he gave Carlton that time but, we all can remember some of them.

I remember the time when he got me real good, too. Mine was for an action that since I've gotten older, I realize deserved. He had to have been feeling something else besides anger when he gave me mine.

Evelyn and I were babysitting or supposedly taking care of our youngest siblings. I know Mama and Daddy had gone to the Crossroads to get groceries. I don't know where everyone else was, but, the baby had been crying and wouldn't stop. I tried to get her to be quiet but she wouldn't. I said, "Either you shut up or I'll drop you in this well!"

She kept yelling. I walked out the back door carrying her to the well. When I got there and put her up on edge of the well. I was telling her to be quiet again when Mama walked up behind me and quietly said, "Eddie, take the baby off the well for me, will you? I need to feed her"

I took her down and told Mama, "Mama, she just wouldn't stop yelling. I told her if she didn't shut I would drop her in that well!"

Then I handed the baby to Mama. She took her in her arms hugging her tightly, patting her on the back and talking to her as she walked into the house

Daddy was there and said. "So she made you mad with her crying? Is that any way to treat your little sister? Do you realize what could have happened while you were holding her over that well?"

"I think you need to come into the kitchen with me for a minute. We need you to understand that you can't put others in danger because you are aggravated."

Daddy took me by the hand and guided me into the kitchen then he put me over his knee and picked up a very flexible little kitchen knife that had no handle on it from the table. He held it by the blade. The knife was very flexible and it became the strap that really **'burned my bottom!'**

When I think back on the incident I realize he didn't hit me too many times but it left a lasting memory. Even with being given some very memorable spankings I still think of my daddy as the best Dad he could be.

Daddy was an active sort of person in our community. He was too much of a friendly kind of person not to be. He did lots of things but I remember that he belonged to the Prince Hall Grand Lodge # 48 of Master Masons. In fact he was an officer. (I know that because he wore the g-square and compass on the apron he usually wore when the Masons were decked-out in their regalia.)

There was also a building next door to Shiloh Baptist Church where they attended their meetings. It was also a place most of the children wanted to get into, but it was always locked.

He was also an active member of the Shiloh Baptist Church and a singer in the choir. He would walk to church with our neighbor Mr. Sam Cornish, a deacon, lot of the times when they went to rehearsals. His being active in the community did not stop his interactions as a loving father with us all the time.

During that time entertainment in our community was at a minimum. But, we had a RCA radio that had a big battery almost the size of a car battery, except it was longer and narrower. Daddy had bought for us. In fact it was the only one for miles around, for a while. We would get many visitors from the community who came by just to enjoy *"The Lone Ranger, Grand Old Opry, Roy Rogers and Dale Evans* on the evenings they came on during the week.

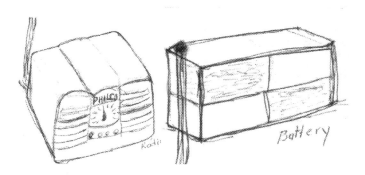

Daddy sometimes would have company over when he was playing barber to the men of the community or repairing their guns or it might also have been the unknown sideline he was said to have been practicing.

Mama and Daddy did other things so that we would not become bored in spite of not allowing us to listen to the radio all the time.

Mama and Daddy provided entertainment themselves if she had to. If there wasn't something in the form of chores that we had to do to get along, Mama recited poetry with expressive drama, and Daddy was the singer. We entertained ourselves as well. Ausie and Carlton somehow learned to play the guitar and Ausie got one from somewhere to accompany some of our family sing-a-longs. Later on all of us sang in the church, as part of a choirs, quartets, and duets or sang solos, except for Ausie and Isiah. Many of us still do.

Some of us can still recite bits of the poems Mama would say. I can only think of a few lines of one that I remember. It goes.....

If Jesus Came To Your House

"If Jesus came to your house to spend a day or two

What would you say, just what in the world would you do?

Would you invite Him in, and think of it as a blessed favor,

Or would you wish He'd gone down the road, to your closest neighbor?"

There was a good bit more to it b ut, after all this time I can only remember a line here and there. I wasn't the only one who remembered times like this and the rhymes she quoted. They were not just once in a while. My sisters can do a much better job of reciting more of her poems than I can.

These recitals were done many times just to entertain us, and other times to keep our minds on what she wanted us to be doing. When were all together in the room most times it was to either entertain or to teach us a lesson.

My sister Evelyn remembers one of her favorites that had to do with Blacks it goes;

What's the name of all you Black Devils?

Yes, it's the name that suits you well.

You are going to drive Billy's cows

Right straight to the gates of hell

Just give you a ripe young virgin

And show you what to do

You'll take and use her

Then just up and leave her when you're through.

Yes, you'll drive Billy's cows right straight

To the gates of hell!

There was a time when I was in the kitchen with Mama when Daddy and the older children were working in what we called the 'old field' and the smaller children were in the yard where she had been washing. She told me to wash the dishes, while she took a bucket from the wash stand, and went to the well. While she was gone I sat down and looked around at the place wishing it looked more like something I had seen in a magazine and wishing I did not have to actually wash the dishes.

Mama stepped back into the kitchen while I was still sitting there daydreaming. She was looking very tired and she was sweating because she had been out back washing (scrubbing clothes in the tin tubs outside, using washboard and P&G soap). She had also been to the garden to get vegetables to fix for everybody to eat later on.

At this time Mama was still in her early thirties, relatively young. Having babies so fast and working so hard seem to make her look healthier and maybe even younger than her age. Though she was plump, she had what black folks considered as fine legs. She also had a face that was quite attractive. She had a lovely smile along with a beautifully soft melodious voice.

She was the kind of person who didn't get angry much, or if she did it didn't show. She made one feel good when they talked with her. On this particular day when she came in and said, "Child, you haven't even started washing those dishes! What's the matter? Can't you make those little hands of yours do anything?"

I felt real bad, this time, that I hadn't done what I was supposed to do, wash the dishes. I said, "Yes Ma'am. Mama, I was thinking. Just wondering really, why we don't have some of the nice pretty furniture like they have in the magazines."

Mama put down the buckets and vegetables came over to me and patted me on the shoulder and said, "Sit down with me honey, your father and all of us work very hard, but we still can't afford that kind of stuff. Maybe one of these days the Lord will fix it so you can have a pretty yard, nice furniture, and all that kind of stuff, ok. Right now we have to be thankful for what He provides. It's enough to supply what we need.

"Now, would you please get busy washing these dishes for Mama, and try to make this kitchen look as nice as you can, huh? Now get busy, will you?"

She patted my cheek, smiled at me then went and poured some dishwater from the stove into the pan for me. (I always knew she loved me but, when she patted my cheek it was like a kiss. I don't remember her kissing any of us after we were past two or so unless we had been away a while. But, the pat on the face was just as fulfilling.)

I washed the dishes and helped her finish cleaning the house. Then she started cooking for the family's next meal, while I went out back into the pasture under the persimmon trees to play with the doll Mama had made for me at Christmas time.

She made dolls from pieces of left over cloth and cotton sacks material (denim) for each of us girls while we were still young enough to play with them. She had sewn on yawn for hair and embroidered a face on the head of the doll. She had also used some old worn out dress material to make a dress for the doll. They were our Christmas presents or gifts for other occasions. Mine was one I loved as much as one could love any doll, maybe more, because I knew Mama made it especially for me.

While I was out playing in my little place under the trees I saw Daddy and my two older brothers coming down the dirt road behind 'the crib', what we called the barn. My Daddy was looking like his old self laughing and talking while they were on their way. I ran out from under the shade trees to meet Daddy.

Zip, the youngest brother, had been over near the tank and came running, too. Willie C. and Carlton went to feed, water, unharnessed the mules and let them out into the pasture.

"Did ya'll finish the plowing in the old field?" Zip wanted to know.

"Yep, we sure did, that's why we got back this early. Y'all will need to help us start chopping the cotton on the new ground tomorrow. I think you two are big enough." Daddy answered him.

"Where's your Mama and everybody else besides you two?"

"Elouise, Evelyn, Laura went somewhere while I was playing I think they went over to Mrs. Metta's and Georgia is in the house with Mama." I told him

We went into the house and Willie C. and Carlton came out of the crib a few minutes later. They went over to the wash bench and washed up for dinner. Mama had us help her set the table, before we began eating her very tasty turnip greens, potatoes, buttermilk, Home cured ham, Cornbread and berry cobbler Mama had cooked for dinner.

We said, as we usually did, a` prayer before starting then while we were eating, they were talking about what needed to be done on the place Mama was just as forthcoming as everyone else.

As we all finished eating. Daddy lit his ever present pipe. We all stayed at the table a few minutes more as we relaxed while he was smoking. We were talking to each other. After a while Daddy got up, got a drink of water out of the bucket near the door and started talking to the boys about cleaning out the crib/barn or some such stuff. Then they went on out the back door.

"The Crib"

I tried to sneak out of the house to follow them as Mama began clearing the table, but she stopped me even without looking in my direction.

Zip snitched, "Mama, call Eddie, she's trying to follow us. We've got work to do and she'll be in the way!"

I gave him an ugly look that he didn't like and he made a jump at me, but I scrambled away. Mama called me back to the kitchen to help her finish cleaning up, the way I was supposed to do in the first place, since the other girls were not there.

On another day Evelyn and I got a chance to have some semi-alone time with Mama because everybody else had something else to do and she allowed us to share a fishing trip to the closest fishing hole closest to the house. We called it 'The Slough.'

We got together the poles and dug some worms, and then we walked across the field and Mr. Sterling Malone's pasture to get there. All the way we were talking about one thing or another. Evelyn and I got to talking about a couple of girls we knew and what we wanted to do to them.

Mama stopped us, "Girls that is no way to talk or to act! You must always act like ladies!"

It was during times like these we got stringent lessons in behavior from her. She told what being like a "lady" meant. "Just being female doesn't make a person, a *lady*. It means the girl/woman follows the things one finds in the Bible *and* act like it. In other words, a *lady* does things to show that there are good things in her heart. She behaves properly and is always expected to dress like one. Her clothes may not be of the best quality or always be the latest style in society. Yet, those clothes should still show that you know *what* the proper thing to wear is and what is not.

"You wouldn't want anyone to think that I didn't care enough about you to teach you how to behave and dress would you?"

"But, Mama," Evelyn asked, "why would anyone think you didn't care about us if we acted badly?"

"They would think that because you are my children. It's my job to teach all of you what is right and what is proper. So you can't just do anything and get away with it. Be nice girls."

"We will, Mama." We both answered.

The fishing trip lasted for hours, to me; it seemed like days I was so bored! I didn't like having to put those grimy, wiggly worms on the hook, and then wait for a bite that might not come, but when it did it was fun. The sitting there waiting quietly so long was the pits! The only good thing about it was time we were alone with Mama and the few fish we caught. (I dislike fishing to this day!)

Ausie the oldest child at home, had been called into service for the United States Army because he gotten old enough. When he was drafted, Mama and Daddy were told, that to be the beneficiaries of his moneys, should anything happen to him, at this time, they had to officially adopt him as a son before he went away to serve in Korea. He spent most of his time in that conflict.

He came home after his service time. He stayed with us again part of the time but he then went to stay and work, most of the time in Dallas.

It was not long after this time that Mama and Daddy welcomed Marvin the youngest child into the world.

He was delivered at home as were all of us, by the midwife Mrs. Florence Vernon. ('Aunt Florence,' to almost everyone I knew in ours and the other surrounding communities). Within a couple of weeks Marvin died.

We never knew what happened other than that he was never quite well from birth. Mama was quieter for a while after his death and the songs, she sang all the time as she worked, were more on the sad side. (I've wondered since that time, especially since I've been a mother, how she managed to keep going and doing all she did. It seemed she was going and doing all the time!) She sewed for the family and the community even with all she had to do for us.

Mama was the kind of seamstress that needed only a picture of the outfit to make it. She had no patterns, nor did she need patterns! People just brought her catalogue cutouts. The fabric was sometimes the printed flour or cornmeal sacks. Most of them brought the fabric themselves or the cornmeal or flour sacks they used back then to be used to make the outfits. She was talented at sewing that's why I think of Mama when reading about Tabitha/Dorcas in the New Testament of the Bible where the people of her community brought items to Peter after she had died to show him of her goodness. That woman, reminds me of Mama. She is listed under two names, one Tabitha in Aramaic, and Dorcas in Greek. She was a disciple of Christ living in Joppa who was full of good works. That was Mama. So many of the people in her community remembered her and told Peter when they summoned him to their city. She made things for the neighbors with her hands. They showed to Peter some of the things she had sewed. Mama's neighbors could have done the same so at that time.

The flour and cornmeal sacks Mama used to produce clothes for her own girls, because she didn't have the money to pay for too much fabric. The fact that the material in the flour or meal sacks didn't matter what did matter was that they were pretty anyway didn't hurt. The dresses she produced were so nice they envied by friends and neighbors. One of my sisters even got bent out of shape at a girl who lived in our community because she got to use one for some special occasion.

What made it so much of a problem for my sister was that the girl in question was thought of by many as a real beauty My sister was not recognized by folks as an equally good looking, or as popular as this girl. This girl got to wear one of my sister's, Mama designed, hand-made, dresses for a special occasion! She has never forgotten the incident!

Mama's sewing was a source of income that the family had to use to help supplement the income needed for such a large family. The

Carlton and some fish

prices she charged were really miniscule when thought of in today's world. But, it helped then in many instances,

At times Daddy even worked on the railroad. For some men in the area he was also a barber for many in the area and, he also did gun repair for them, too. There was a **rumor** that he had another hidden popular illegal sideline. It was only speculation; I saw no evidence of it.

Daddy was one who really loved to fish which he did as often as he could. He would go, and even at times, stay all night. When he came home with a large catch Mama would have us help clean them and then share some with the neighbors.

I can remember the memorable time Daddy and the older boys went fishing and came home after being gone all night.

They brought home a ton of fish. The girls as usual had the job of cleaning. The brothers had some tales to tell about how they had to wrestle about two hours when they caught one very big fish and the catching of some of the others. The boys had the job of cleaning the big fish and cutting it up. When the cleaning and cutting of the fish was done we were sent in different directions to share it with the other neighbors.

We had fish for dinner that evening then sat down to listen to Daddy and the boys tell more tales of their fishing trip. We all stayed up a while later listening to them. Daddy and Mama decided that it was time for them to go to bed. We went into the kitchen to talk. While we were talking we heard a loud noise like someone had fallen in our parents' room.

We all rushed into the room and found Daddy on the floor. He was unconscious.

Mama had jumped out of the bed and begun patting his face; she then rushed to get a wet wash cloth and rubbed his face with it until his eyes came open. He tried to speak but nothing came out. He couldn't talk!

Mama began to cry. She kept calling out to him, "Mr. Will, Mr. Will! What's the matter?"

She looked at Carlton with tears running down her face, "Carlton, run as fast as you can to Metta's and Sterling's. Son please hurry I have no idea what is wrong with your father!"

"Willie C., help me put him back into the bed."

"Elouise, find me something to put on your father."

By this time Mama seem to be in control of hers emotions. She then turned to the rest of us because we were all standing around the bed after she and Willie C. had gotten him back in the bed, and told us, "Now, all of you go into the kitchen I'll have to dress your father so we can take him to the doctor. I'm sure he'll be all right, ok?"

We all went back into the kitchen, but this time we were all very quiet.

Elouise came back after getting everything for Mama and sat down with us. Mama sat holding Daddy's hand while we waited for Mr. Sterling and Mrs. Metta to come and help her get Daddy to the doctor. She also kept bathing his face with the damp towel.

After a few minutes, that seemed like hours to us, Mr. Sterling and Mrs. Metta drove up. They rushed into the house. Mrs. Metta was saying as she came in the door, "Babe, Babe, is Mr. Will all right?"

Mama told them as quickly as she could what had happened and asked, "Could ya'll help me get him to the hospital?"

"You know we will do everything we can, Babe. Boys, come over here and let's get you Daddy into the car."

Mr. Sterling told my brothers. They picked Daddy up as gently as they could and got him into the back seat of the car. Mrs. Metta and Mama got in and they drove off.

We sat around quite stunned for a while then Elouise told us, "We may as well go to bed because there was nothing we can do sitting around here. Maybe we will hear something soon."

About nine the next morning Mama sent word by Mr. Sterling that Daddy had had a stroke and was paralyzed completely on his right side. She told us not to worry even though he would be in the hospital for a while. She also asked that we send her some things that both she and Daddy needed.

Mama stayed at the hospital for two days before being able to come home again. When she did come, she was very tired and sleepy. Her feet were also swollen. But she called us all together and said, "Ya'll, your Daddy as I sent word to you the other day had a stroke and is paralyzed on his right side. He'll have to be in the hospital for some time. I'm going to try and be with him as much as I possibly can.

"You all will have to be here by yourselves. I want all of you to try and be very good and obey Elouise and Carlton. I know they are not much older than some of you, but I have to leave them in charge because they are the oldest. I don't like leaving ya'll like this but I just don't know what else to do.

"The doctor said that if you father can get some exercise he may be able to walk again but because of his age they are not sure.

"Now if there is anything you need, go over to Lula and Tracy's. They will let me know when Lula comes to see Mr. Will.

"Is there anything ya'll want to ask me before I go try and get a little nap?"

Evelyn asked for us, "Mama when can we go up there and see Daddy?"

"Elouise, Carlton, and Willie C. are the only ones who can come on Saturday. The rest of you are too young and they won't let you in the hospital. You know you have to be twelve years old to go into the hospital room."

"Mama, can Daddy talk now?" I asked.

"Not really. He still can't speak clearly." Mama answered.

Someone wanted to know, "Did the doctor say when he would be able talk clearly again?"

"No, he didn't," was all the answer Mama could give him.

Then Carlton got up and said, "All right ya'll, those are all the questions Mama need to hear right now. She need to get some sleep." and shooed us out of the room.

Mama went back to the hospital later that evening. She had to spend almost three months there with Daddy before they allowed him to come home. When he did come home he didn't know anybody but Mama. He didn't call any of us by our own names. He called me either Cardelia or Lula. When they came to see him he didn't know them at all for some time.

Mama continued to give him the exercises the doctor recommended and he slowly began to learn to walk all over again. In the meantime he learned to talk better again, too. He still insisted on calling us girls at home by the two older ones names.

This had a bad affect on one of my sisters. She was a bit afraid of him because his eyes were not as focused as they were before the stroke. They were crossed a bit. She became nervous and jittery around him, especially since he would become quite agitated and would talk very loudly. I toughened it out even enough to feed him since he couldn't feed himself for awhile. There were times when he was worse than a baby when he tried.

The extra doctor bills and the bills for medicine caused problems for Mama and the family. During the time of the year when the chopping of cotton came, all the children who were old enough were going places to work. I was not quite old enough Daddy told me. But, I think it was because I had been helping him out and Mama needed me to help her with the younger children; Zip, Laura, Georgia and Lean.

When the cotton picking time came that fall I begged Daddy to let me go with my older brothers and sisters and let my sister stay and help Mama. I thought it would be more fun than staying home.

While we were gone my sister and Daddy really fell out. Daddy seemed so happy to see me. When I came in he said, "Cardelia, (using my oldest sister's name) don't you ever leave me again, your sister can't find anything! Did you know she couldn't even find my cane when it was right over there by the door?"

He then asked me, "How did you enjoy yourself while you were gone?

"Daddy I was able to pick between a 100-150 pounds of cotton a day."

When I talked to my sister afterwards I found out that even though my sister was just a *little* afraid of Daddy when we left her home to help Mama with Daddy, when we returned she was really afraid of him.

She told me when we were off by ourselves, "Before Daddy would ask for something I would know exactly where it was, but if he asked me to get it, I would not able to find it to save my life! He makes me a nervous wreck!"

After the cotton picking season was over that year we had paid of some of the heaviest bills. Mama was able to put a little aside for later as we all went back to school. She had become the head of the house after his stroke. She let us know that she was struggling to make ends meet. She had never had to do this kind of thinking before. She had always turned that kind of things over to whoever her husband was.

She was really glad because Daddy was attempting some activities. She wasn't too worried about his health while he felt he could do some things on his own.

It was at this time Daddy had a serious talk with Carlton and Willie C. One of those kinds of talks about being men and doing all they could to take care of the family one day. He took ill the very next day.

My sister Georgia Mae says she remembers as if it were a dream, being on an adventure with Daddy when it happened. She and Lean went on a walk to Shiloh Church with Daddy to see how the construction on the building of our new church building was going. He used stories and jokes to keep them entertained as they walked there because it took them quite a while to make the trip. On the way back from the church is when he probably had the stroke that sent him to the hospital for the last time.

As they were coming back across the creek down from Aunt Georgia's house, Daddy went down. He had been teasing them about whether or not they could run and how far they could go since both were very young About 4 and 3 years old). When he fell, he told them, "I bet you can't run all the way to your Aunt Georgia Ann's house up the trail."

Thinking he was playing another game with them, they told him, "Oh yes we can, too!"

"Lean can you run, too?" Daddy asked.

Lean answered eagerly, "Yeah, Daddy, I run."

"Then, Georgia, catch hold of Lean's hand run as fast as you can to her house and tell her to come here," Daddy told them.

When they got to Aunt Georgia's house she was in the yard and asked them, "Where is Buddy? Wasn't he with you two?"

Georgia Mae answered for them. "Daddy says for you to come to down to the creek, where he is. He fell down when got there."

Aunt Georgia told them to get the message to Mama and the others at the house. So they ran there and told Mama.

It was a day in March. Sister Lula's husband, Tracy, came to the school and to let us know that Daddy had been taken back to the hospital. He was one of the school bus drivers.

We all left and went back home before school let out. It was later on that evening that Mama sent us word that Daddy was resting all right but, he was under sedation. The doctors said that he had suffered another stroke. From the way Tracy gave us Mama's message, he gave the opinion that they didn't expect Daddy to live.

In fact, that same night Mama sent some of the neighbors who were there- to our house to get the older children to come to the hospital to see Daddy. The doctor thought that it was better to come if they wanted to see him alive. That left me and all the children who were younger than me at home. We were not the right age.

When they all got back that night/early the next morning they were all really hopeful that Daddy would be all right in spite of what the doctor had said. They said that Daddy knew them and he was talking when they left the hospital that morning.

That next day, on the morning of March 25, 1948, he passed away after they had seen him. Mama was in the hospital room with him. She told us what happened that morning.

"Babe, Daddy said quietly, "What were all those children doing here that time of night?"

She told him, "They came because they wanted to see you and it is hard to get anyone to drive them up her at this time of the year when everyone is trying to get their crops planted and their fields plowed. You know that. They came when they could."

"Babe, you know you never could lie real good." Daddy said to her smiling at her all the time.

"Those children were here because the doctor told you I would not live until morning, didn't he?"

"Now Mr. Will, where in the world did you get an idea like that, you are still here aren't you?" Mama asked looking quickly away as she went to his bed to straighten the covers that were already straight.

"All right Babe, Daddy said raising his good hand weakly, "I just asked but, both you and I know the real truth. I could tell by the way the kids looked at me."

"Mr. Will I don't know..."

"That's all right, I won't say anything more. I am going to sleep. You had better get some sleep too, Babe, you've been up two nights in a row without sleep."

"Mr. Will, will you stop worrying about me. I am all right. Will you just try and get some rest?"

"First I think you ought to go for a short walk first. Then I'll feel better."

"I don't think walking outside will help me. I'm all right Just get some rest for me."

"I'll get some rest, Babe, "if do one thing for me."

"What is that, Mr. Will?"

"Lay over there on that bed and let me see you go to sleep," Daddy answered pointing to the extra bed they had put into the room for Mama.

"All right, Mr. Will, "You win I'll go to sleep but, you will call me if you need something, won't you?"

"Yeah, yeah, I'll do that now get some sleep, please?"

Mama lay down and pretended to go to sleep. Through partially closed eyes she saw Daddy raised up on his good arm to see if she was asleep. When he saw that her eyes seemed to be closed he started to lie back down in the bed and she heard him make a funny noise in his throat. She jumped up from the bed and ran over to him.

She noticed that something was wrong; she took him in her arms and called to him. "Mr. Will, Mr. Will!"

He opened his eyes opened after and said weakly, "Ba....be, Ba....be I... thought... you ...were...slee..." Then he slumped onto the bed.

"Mr. Will! Mr. Will! O Lord he's gone! Mr. Will, what am I going to do?"

That evening after they had taken Daddy to the morgue, Mama came home looking tired and drawn but strangely calm and but, stiff. She had told everyone not to tell us that Daddy was dead until she got home. She would tell us herself. Even though we didn't know what had happened we knew something was wrong because of the way Mama looked.

She called us all together in the kitchen around the table there. After she had thanked Tracy for bringing her home and he drove off.

"Children, she began, "this will probably be no shock to you, but your father is gone. There were complete silence for a few seconds then Elouise broke the silence with a loud piercing scream. "No! Daddy, Daddy, Daddy!"

At this point most of us began sobbing brokenly.

"Children, Mama said, "I am sure your Father would not want us to carry on like this. Let's just remember that he suffered a great deal these past few months. Now he is at rest. We will just have to try and do the best we can without him. Right now we have to think of the funeral. Carlton, you will have to go to Lula's and tell her to get in touch with Mr. Will's Sister in Dallas and his brothers in Oklahoma. I'll tell Mrs. Georgia myself.

The day of the funeral dawned cloudy and grey. Daddy's two brothers, their wives and younger sister, Amy, were at our house. I have no idea why it came to me then but, they were nothing like my daddy. They really seemed like strangers to me, even though I had seen them before.

The way they talked about the things Daddy liked so much as if it they were detestable. Uncle P. C. said he didn't like this part of the country, and Uncle Ed thought living here was not something he would want to do. They both thought nothing of telling Mama they didn't see how she and Daddy made it.

"Sister, why on earth did you and Buddy ever settle in this part of the country?" Uncle P. C. asked her.

"Your brother and I both liked it here." Mama answered calmly.

"What is there here to like? There is nothing in sight but a bunch of trees and fields!" Uncle Ed told her.

"Mr. Will and I both liked those trees and the fields. They were ours."

"P.C., come in here and get your clothes on so we can go!" That was his wife Jewel calling to him.

"Yes dear, I'm coming!" He answered.

We all then got ready for the funeral. The family car picked up Mama and my older sisters brothers. There was not enough room in the one family car for all of us, so some of us rode in cars with other family members and neighbors.

I learned at the funeral how much the people in our area thought of my father. They even turned out school for the funeral!

I had never heard of something like this happening before. Another thing I noticed was the number of flowers that were all over the front of the church. The minister said so many great things about my daddy as well as other members of the church who got up and made complimentary remarks about him. The funeral was so sad for all of the family. It seemed to take ages.

They were not able to have the funeral at our home church because it was still under construction. It was held at Owen Chapel Church of God in Christ. We had to be taken over to Shiloh Church to the cemetery that had been donated to the church by Daddy years earlier.

After this time Mama, really had to take charge. I am sure she was really felt she was swamped. She was on 38 years old with the responsibility of nine minor children! She was feeling, I am sure, inundated with stuff needing find a way for survival!

The only experience she had had at being in charge, were the months when Daddy was incapacitated with the first stroke, but at least he was there for her to talk to about what was troubling her.

Now she was on her own.

She was the Best Mama

From the date and time of my birth she was there for me
She helped me to grasp things I'd never have otherwise been able to see
The lessons she taught me and all my sisters and brothers
Came with examples of how to live with and treat others
Though we were awfully poor and had so little
She did well teaching us God's Word, trying not to leave out one jot or tittle.

After Daddy's death the family went through some pretty rough times. There were times when we had not one piece of bread to eat or the where withal to get any. There were times we went without bread but Mama continued on. Mama would manage to scrape up something around the farm but, there was no bread. No flour or meal was to be had. We ate potatoes in place of bread. Mama's word of comfort during these times was that we would make it because the 'Lord would provide'.

Daddy had been the strong one in the marriage, and he handled all of the business. He had never bothered to tell Mama anything about how to take care of things connected with business. Mama became so frustrated and confused about what to do. There was no chance to learn neither in school nor in her prior marriage or her second with Daddy,

My Sister Lula's husband, Tracy, began to help her take care of some of the business. Whenever Mama needed advice on how or what was to be done about something many times she would ask him. For a while there were a lot of things to be taken care.

Mama used the meager insurance and Daddy's lodge coverage to bury him and to pay off the mortgage on the land and live on.

After that was done the land was divided. Mama had the court to divide the land into equal parts for all Daddy's children, except his daughter Edie. Since she hadn't *legally* been identified as his daughter, even though he had raised her the law didn't count her as one of his children. Mama took none of the land for herself. She even allowed Cardelia, Lula and Ausie their choice for their share of the property, and only took the guardianship rights of the property for the nine minor children still at home what was left. She only kept for herself the right to live on the property for as long as she lived. She asked for nothing else for herself.

Mama then had the responsibility of caring for all of us and the business of the household.

After all this was done not all of the debts had been paid. Mama didn't even know that we owed

them. As stated before, Mama asked Uncle Tracy to help her with details. For this he had to come over to the house a lot more often than was usual. Then one day Aunt Lula came over herself and she looked upset.

"Babe, I'd like to talk to talk to you!" She said a bit angrily.

"Hi, Lula, "How are you? Come into the house won't you?" Mama asked her.

"Babe, you know we have always been friends every since you and Daddy married." She told Mama.

"Yes, that's right Lula why do you ask?" Mama asked worriedly.

"Well Babe, I've heard some very disturbing things about you and Tracy."

Mama looked so shocked and hurt. She asked Lula, "What did you hear, Lula?"

"I know you don't want me to repeat that, in front of these children!" She said tightly."I'd rather talk to you alone, if you don't mind."

"All right, just give me a minute. Evelyn, will you take the children outside to the barn?" Mama told my sister.

"Yes Ma'am, She answered. "Come on ya'll let's go outside and play a while."

"All right, Lula, now what is it?" I heard Mama say as she closed the door. I don't know what Mama and Aunt Lula said to each other but, after that Mama and Lula was still friends, but Tracy didn't come to the house to help Mama anymore.

After Daddy's death Mama's strength was really put to the test. She now had Ausie, and nine other minor children at home to be clothed and fed. She alone was head of the household. She had to step up to the plate.

Mama lost a lot of weight during this time. (Thinking about it, since that time and remembering that Mama had only a third grade education and she had been having, and caring for, children from the age of seventeen years old it is not surprising that she was having such s bad time.) Her loss of weight only had her looking even more attractive!

After Daddy's death something happened that I didn't learn the meaning of until much later in life. It was connected to that something rumored about in the community that I had no idea of, first because I was too young to realize and secondly that I didn't *want* to know.

Ausie and Carlton were in the woods doing something when Mama got a broom and went into the woods. When they came back Ausie and Carlton were grimacing and giggling. Mama didn't look her usual calm, smiley faced. They, I understood from later knowledge, were trying to make bootleg liquor back in the woods behind the house. Mama let them know in no uncertain terms that she would not tolerate that kind of thing on any of the property.

Ausie being of age soon moved to Dallas.

After Daddy's passing there was a noticeable difference in the visitors who came by the house. Mama' reaction to them was just the same. But a lot of the bachelors of the community, and a few others men, especially began to come by our house for one thing or another. But, Mama paid no more attention to them than she did when Daddy was alive. She would smile and treat them the same as usual.

After a while the parade began to slow down considerably. But, many people in the community didn't see things quite the same way about Mama. For some reason the women were always asking Mama when she expected to get married again!

"I don't expect to get married again. I have too many children to ask any man to take care of." She would answer. Yet, somehow it didn't to curb the speculation or that question.

Mama's help as a seamstress even went away after the talk and rumors had started. Mama never seemed to give up though, she continued to repeat he favorite saying, "The Lord will provide."

Mama did her best to continue teaching each of us the right things to do in every situation she could think of us getting into. There was one thing though she did not get into. She was like so many parents are even today. *She did not talk about sex.* She did not feel comfortable talking as explicitly as some of us have to do today because of the dangers out there. Her message to each of us girls was mostly, "Keep your legs closed and your dress down!

She was very on point when she would talk about how one ought to live, treat one's fellowman and doing all the good for everyone you could. She also taught us to be liberal givers to the Lord's work, especially to the church. She would say, "What the church officers do with it you can't control. The motives that are in your heart for giving money, your time or your things should be to help others and to do your duty for the cause of Christ, only."

She showed us by her actions, as well as her words that reading and getting familiar with God's Word (The Bible) had to be an integral part of what a Christian must do. Though she had only had a third grade education, she read The Bible constantly. She would read it audibly because this was the best way she could understand what she read. Many of the words she had to spell aloud, over and over again to be able to pronounce or understand what was said or meant.

Mama was also a woman of prayer! She made it obvious for all her children and guest who stayed in our house to see, and hear. You see, Mama prayed **every** night and day especially, as she prepared for bed no matter where we were. Her prayers were also done audibly.

I personally took some of the words from her prayers to use in my own prayers when I was learning to pray. It was a while before I realized she was praying for me and my other siblings. I've learned that I did what so many folk do first. I wasn't just talking to my Lord and Savior I was saying what, **I** thought, <u>sounded</u> like a good prayer. I noticed she would **always,** ask the Lord, to either take care of or bless the "off-springs" of her body. It sounded good when she said it. (I did too until I decided to lookup offspring and learned the definition of the word.) I knew we were supposed to be praying because she would talk to us often about praying to God and also depending on him to be there.

Mama was an excellent cook! Her homemade biscuits, teacakes, and other much loved dishes brought joy to all of her children as well community folks who had the chance to partake of it. There were times we only had that good flour gravy Mama could make, and her biscuits. Sometimes when we went to bed I'm sure she may not have had any idea what we were going to eat the next day! However, by daybreak she'd be up before sunrise to rig up the very best meal she could obtain to place before the family. Her excellent biscuits were done superbly, even though she may not have had all the things the recipe called for. Somehow she would pull it off. After Daddy died she had to pull of some miracles in order for us to make it. And, she did!

Mama didn't have a driver's license and neither did anyone else who lived at home after Ausie left. She had to hire someone to drive Daddy's car whenever we had to go someplace. I noticed that whenever she got a man who was married to drive us or her someplace for more than once she would not get him to drive any more.

One day I heard my sister, Elouise   ask her about this. "Mama, why don't you get some of the men who used to drive for us anymore?"

"Well Elouise, if I could, I would drive myself and us where we need to go but, your father never got around to showing me how to drive and I don't know who to get to teach me now because all the supposedly respectable men I get to take us or me anywhere end up trying to get me to lower my dignity and do something I refuse to do, or some of the ladies of the community think I'm going to take it upon myself and ask them to.... O' well, let's just say that the life of a widow under 40 isn't an easy one." It didn't remain a problem long because the old jalopy didn't last very long. It just stopped working, especially since it was said to have been held together with spit, nails and bailing wire.

About a year or two after Daddy passed away Mama came home and told us that with the money that Ausie had sent us while he was in the service and the money she had saved from the policy Daddy had had, we were going to able to build us a new home!

She was really excited about the prospect of our having a new house. She said, "If only your father were alive to enjoy this home with us."

It was the first time I had seen Mama cry since the time she told us about Daddy being dead.

After they began the house we had to move into the Wilson house up the road from our old house. It was an experience staying there, because first of all, it had a fire place in it and we had not had one before, nor had we had the room for one. We were closer to the road that led to the school and the Crossroad where we bought our groceries.

We were also more accessible to the men who wanted to make Mama a girlfriend. It didn't work any better for them this time than it had before. They stopped coming a while except for one or two men. Mr. Willie was one of the one who continued to hang around for a while. He would come on his horse. They would go into the room and talk to each other alone. She had not done that with many men. But, after while he even stopped coming. Mama continued on as usual.

One friend that Mama had during all this time was Mrs. Metta Malone. She seemed to treat Mama the same in spite of what must have been going on in the community. Mrs. Metta continued to quietly be there whenever needed. She was not one for talking a lot but she and Mama seemed to relate to each other. They were friends until Mrs. Metta was gone.

The decision by Mama to build got underway. She got Reverend L. C. McIlveen, the pastor of Shiloh Baptist church, to present the plans and build the house. He had the help of my brothers with the building so Mama would be able to pay for the whole thing. She even had to have them use some of the good lumber from the old house to complete the new one.

It was finally finished and we were able to move in. It was not all that much larger than the old one but, it was enough to make it different and very much appreciated! In it there was a separate kitchen and dining room, a living room/bedroom for the girls and another bedroom for my brothers. The other bedroom was Mama's room. There was a wood heater that was used for keeping us warm in the winter in that room. That room was also where the family gathered.

During all this time Mama continued to lose weight because she was so stressed, too. The responsibility of the family at home, the length of Daddy's illness, his death and, I surmised later, that some of the tension she was under had to do with all the rumors going around. All this took a real toll on Mama. It caused such a strain that Mama had to be taken to the hospital with stress, fatigue and a full nervous breakdown. We had to rush her to the hospital after she had gone to bed with a terrible headache. Sister Lula came and stayed with us for most of the day after Mama was taken to the hospital. She kept saying, "I knew it was going to happen to Babe! She has been working too hard. And all that talk and all those lies going around did not help her one bit."

"What talk, Aunt Lula?" Evelyn asked her.

"All the talk that been going around about your mama, that has kept her so stressed, it has made her sick! That's, what talk!"

Mama was in the hospital for about three weeks. Then she was brought home for a while. The doctors then told her she needed to get away for a while. They didn't know what was bothering her but something was.

Mama's two older sons, Otis and Cotis came to our house and took Mama to Dallas where they lived for the care, and some rest time she needed. They also said she would be close to a doctor at all times.

After a long discussion which included Mama, She finally agreed to go, but with the understanding that it would only be as long as she needed extra care.

When they got her to Dallas they were not able to keep her with them they took her to live with Aunt Sis, her sister, and her family in Grand Prairie, Texas.

Aunt Sis, Arlean Green

Once in Dallas, when my brothers took Mama to see a doctor, all I was told, is that he looked foreign.

"His comments to Mama when he came into the room were so way off the mark!" My oldest brother was especially bothered, even talking to me about it after so many years.

After looking at her for a minute, the doctor said, "What can I do for you today? Honey, you know what I think, I think you need is a man!"

That made my brothers really steam, and it had the same effect on my other brothers later when they told them what the doctor had said.

My brother said Mama made no response to him, and then he said "Let's see what we can do for you."

Even though they left her in the office with him, my brothers were really ticked. My oldest brother Otis's comment was, "He really made me mad, even though he seemed to have been a good doctor, from all we had heard of him, before we took her there.

"We continued to take her there in spite of being quite upset at him. Mama didn't seem to be bothered by him. She did get better seeing him awhile. I still, even today, have problems with his comments!"

I didn't personally learn of this incident until this writing. While this was happening the rest of us were involved with our own dramas at home.

We were left at the house Mama had just had built. Mama felt Carlton and Elouise would be able to handle things until she was able to return. That didn't have time to prove to be the case. Something happened that made it different.

We were there for a few weeks actually as we waited to hear from Mama. We did alright until there was a mix-up about our getting groceries at the crossroads.

We had credit at Mr. Mimn Woods's Grocery store. We were able to get food we needed from the store until there was some mix-up in who was to do it, and how much were could get.

(Sister) Aunt Lula was involved, Mr. Mimn said that she told him she had the right to get our

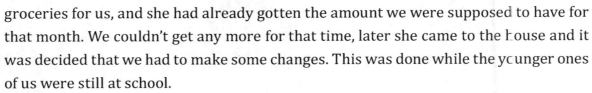

groceries for us, and she had already gotten the amount we were supposed to have for that month. We couldn't get any more for that time, later she came to the house and it was decided that we had to make some changes. This was done while the younger ones of us were still at school.

Aunt Lula decided to have the sisters stay with her in her home on school days but we would go home with our brothers for the weekends. This had to do with the mix up about the money the government was providing for our care that was to be given to Mr. Mimn for our groceries and who was supposed to get our groceries.

Elouise went home with her. Those of us who were at school came home from school one day and were met by Aunt Lula with instructions of what we were to do. We, the girls, were going to stay with her at her home while the boys would stay at home.

The boys . . . Carlton, Willie C and Zip would have to manage at the house because there was not enough room for them at her house.

I have no idea how long this arrangement lasted but, one day during that time we came home from school and Aunt Lula told us as we came in, "Lue Willie would you go with Margaret Nell, Laura, and Eddie to pick those plums over by the woods before they are gone?

Norma, you, Elouise Evelyn, Obra Faye,

Rachel and take Bessie with you, ya'll are to go and finish picking the peas in the field next to the church."

"Aunt Lula, did we get any mail from Mama today?" I asked.

"No, you didn't, now go get out of those school clothes and get to work." Lula told me.

"Tracy, what are you waiting for? Why don't you get those girls and take them over so they can get to work before it get dark. Besides I'd like to begin the canning tomorrow." Aunt Lula told him.

We all finished getting ready in a few minutes; Aunt Lula seemed to be in a real mood. We all went our different directions.

Lue Willie asked me as we were going out to the orchard, "Why do you think Mer'dear is in such a grouchy mood?"

"I don't know." I told her.

"When do you think ya'll, will be going home or where Cousin Babe is?"

"I don't know that either, but I hope it will be soon. I would like to know how she is doing." I told her as the others went on ahead.

"I wonder what I made on that test the teacher gave us, today." I asked her.

"Oh I think I did all right," She said winking her eye at me. "You probably did well, you usually do and I have a good chance that that I got a good one, too."

"Uncle Tracy, should we pick the half ripe ones to or just the ripe ones?" I called to him, as he was by then on the other side of the orchard where from Lue Willie and I were working. The others with us were working on the trees down a ways from us.

"I think since Lula plans to can them tomorrow, we ought to just pick ripe one for this trip. Ok?" He answered and began whistling.

We picked plums for the rest of the evening. Then we went to the house for dinner when it began to get dark. Aunt Lula met us at the door. "Did ya'll finish picking all those plums?"

"Most of them," Uncle Tracy answered her.

"Tracy, do you have any gas in the car? I think we need to go to the store." she told him.

"Yes Lula, you told me this morning before I took the bus out that we might need to get some," Uncle Tracy told her as he went into the house.

As we all came in, Aunt Lula told Norma, "Rachel, will you girls check to make sure everything is ready for everyone to eat, then see that the younger ones are ready for bed. It is a little late for them."

"Aunt Lula, Elouise asked, "Did our check come in today?"

"Why, Elouise? Do you plan on buying something special with it?" She asked her.

"No, Aunt Lula, but Mama told me that Lean needed a pair of shoes." Elouise told her.

After Aunt Lula gone out the door to the car, Uncle Tracy looked out first, and whispered to Elouise, "I think Lula did get a letter today in the mail I don't know what it was."

"But, you heard her, Uncle Tracy. She acted as if she knew nothing about it!"

"Well, I think she got it anyway. But, you know your sister."

Elouise stared at the door he went out of for a moment as if puzzled then she went into the kitchen to help Rachel and Faye with the preparing of the evening meal. I just happened to be in the room next to them.

Later that night after we had all finished dinner and were about to prepare for bed, Aunt Lula and Uncle Tracy came in. They brought with them a lot of groceries and other items including a pair of little shoes for Lean.

"Elouise, you don't have to worry about going to ya'll's house to get too many more things. I think we can make it with what we already have here. Aunt Lula told her. "Now, Tracy, take the rest of the things out of the car."

After I had overheard what Uncle Tracy had told Elouise, I was sure that Aunt Lula had gotten our check and spent it. Aunt Lula turned toward me and said, "Eddie, would you mind staying here tomorrow with Elouise and me to take care of the babies since I have the canning I need to do?"

I was feeling quite angry with my sister by then, so my answer was not very congenial. I said, "Yes, Lula I would Mind! I want to go to school tomorrow so I can get my test results and do the makeup exam Mr. Bryant said I needed for those days I have already missed out of school because Mama was sick."

When I finished speaking Aunt Lula just stared at me for a minute. Then she exploded. "What do you mean you would **mind** staying here tomorrow?"

"I mean, Lula, I answered back insolently, "that I have already missed a number of days out of school as it is and I would not like to miss anymore. I already had to stay in third grade because I was absent too much!"

"Well, what's with you calling me Lula? Ya'll don't usually call me that. Is it that you think you are getting grown, young lady?"

"You are my sister aren't you?" I asked.

"Yes, but you haven't ever called me Lula before! Why the sudden change?"

"Well, I just felt like it. If you can take our money and spend it like you wish without telling us about it. I think I have the right to call you anything I please. Don't you?"

looked at me for a moment without saying a word then turned and left the room.

"Eddie, was that a way to talk to Lula? Uncle Tracy asked me. "Why did you?"

"Because, Uncle Tracy she asked for it, spending our money and telling Elouise she hadn't gotten our check. Not asking anyone about it. She was the one who insisted that we stay with ya'll! Aunt Georgia would have probably have stayed with us at our own house if we had asked her since she doesn't have any one else. We would have had more room than we have here!"

Elouise spoke up for Aunt Lula saying, "Maybe Aunt Lula just wanted to take care of us herself."

"No, she didn't, Lula never volunteered to do anything for anyone unless there was something in it for her. Our check was the prize she got this time!"

Aunt Lula came back into the room. We stared at each other for a few seconds. Then she said, "I was just trying to help. Besides, there are enough groceries there for all of us. Ya'll are staying here so we all will have something to eat."

"Were you trying to help us, Dear Sister, when you caused Mama to come out with none of Daddy's land after she worked to help buy it all those years?" I asked her.

"Just what do you mean by that, Eddie?" Aunt Lula asked darkly.

"Well **Sister** Lula, who was it that argued so much that Mama decided to give all of the land to us in equal share's and forget about herself to keep down confusion when Daddy died, Huh?"

"Eddie, get in that room and go to bed before I forget you are too young to know what you are talking about!" Aunt Lula said seeming ready to explode.

I looked her straight in the eye for several seconds longer. She saw that I was too mad to even be frightened, even after she screamed at me where everyone in the house could hear her. She seemed to fold up.

Then she said to me in a tired voice, "Eddie, you are something else! Huh, I am sorry, she said after a minute. I guess we are both upset. You, about you mother, and yes, I do feel guilty about spending ya'll's check!"

Uncle Tracy looked at her as if he were a bit puzzled.

Aunt Lula saw him look at her and she told him, "Yes, Tracy I did get their check. I cashed and spent some of the money. I wanted to keep Eddie here tomorrow to help Elouise so I could go to town tomorrow before the canning, and pay off some more of our bills."

"Eddie you can go to school tomorrow." She told me as she saw I was going to speak up, again.

After that night Aunt Lula went out of her way to be extra kind to me. It was because of that stupid check and the confusion that it caused that we all hoped never to be in that position again.

Evelyn told me, when I talked about it, we even made a pact to work hard enough that we would not to ever get to where we would have to depend on welfare ever again.

The letter we had been hoping for finally came. It was telling us that Mama was much better! She had been released from the doctors' constant supervision and care since she was staying with Aunt Sis.

Arlean Green, Mama's sister

They had also found an apartment there in Grand Prairie where she felt she could care for her own family again. The place they found  was also not far from Aunt Sis and her family. It was a on a street called either Spike or Sherman, I am not sure which.

These are the names my brothers, it was. What they did say was that we on the other, and the fact that it was sister and my cousin said they thought lived on one of them and Aunt Sis lived very close to Aunt Sis.

One of Mama's other sisters Aunt were not too far away since she also in Fort Worth. Aunt Lellure and her they wanted us to stay there to make Nola and Uncle Lorenzo Edwards lived in Dallas. Uncle Artis Hayes lived family still lived in Vernon. I think sure Mama was able to handle a family

Nola Edwards

before she took on the job at home by herself.

When we got to Grand Prairie, were we so glad to see Mama! She looked so good to all of us. We were all so excited. We had never live in the city before. Along with being able to be with Mama again, it was mind-blowing to see that she was so much better than she had been when she had left us. She was more like her old self again. She was back to reading the Bible aloud and singing as she did most things and being busy most of the time. She also had her Mona Lisa smile back!

She was a bit tenuous about our being out on the city streets. She did all she could to keep us within the apartment especially at night. There were many times she would let us entertain ourselves with whatever we could get into. Then there were times when she felt that we needed to be kept away from some event or activity that was going on and we, thought we ought to be allowed to go. She got back into the habit of doing her dramatic poems.

Georgia, one of my youngest sisters, remembers a few of the words of one she would say in particular.

"Mama, Mama, come here come quick!
God has gone to bed and has not put out His candlestick.

Sh..sh..sh hush child," the mother said.
God does not get tired like us
Nor He does need to sleep
He sits up all through the night
His loving watch over us He keeps keep."

Her efforts were to keep us on the right track, too, even if we were in a city. Knowing the difference from what we were used to, she would involve us in as many activities inside that she could think up that were wholesome.

The city was new experience for all of us. Almost everything was so absolutely different. We were most certainly glad to be around some of our other family, since we got to really know some of our other cousins. We stayed in the apartment Mama and Aunt Sis had gotten for us yet we were able see them often. Since they were just a street or two away. We lived there for, I believe, about three months and a few weeks. We attended the schools there till the end of the year. It was a real enlightening experience for us all.

Zip, our baby brother at the time, was about ten or eleven. He recalls being rather a rambunctious fellow, like he was for many years. He liked to go about getting into stuff. He relates an incident about himself with an old bicycle he got from somewhere. It had rims with no tires on it. He had to pump really hard just to make it even roll on those rims. Yet, he rode it *against* Mama's expressed wishes and instructions.

One day he had been, on a busy street called Jefferson near the downtown strip, also a place where he was told not to go. He was going down another street toward the railroad tracks when he somehow collided with a car. He got knocked up on the hood of the automobile. He was miraculously unhurt, by the car!

Mama was some upset with him! After she found out his body was completely unbroken by the accident, she made sure he hurt somewhere else. She gave him a very good whipping with an electric cord to make sure he got the message about not disobeying her about something as dangerous as riding recklessly on a broken bicycle in the streets. This is just one of the incidents of misbehavior Mama had to deal with there, there were many more I am sure, that I don't recall.

While we were there we also went to church, sometimes with Aunt Sis and her family at the Saint John Baptist Church and sometimes to the Church of God in Christ that was only a little ways from where our apartment was located.

Evelyn says, as a teenager, she remembers being able to get her first job as a waitress. She got it at an eating place not too far from where our apartment was. She worked long enough buy herself a new pink dress. She also remembers loving it tremendously. She had to give up the job after she got sick, since, Mama thought that her working there was part of the reason she was sick. She was not too comfortable with her working there anyway.

We all got to find out what it was like living with a large family in the city. It was so much different from living in the country. The people were different from the people at home and a bit strange to us, at times. We all had a few memorable experiences.

I personally got to like some of them and the school a great deal. In fact I enjoyed school. On my first day at the new school, the teacher introduced me to the class of students who would be in my homeroom for the rest of the year. Frankly I was a bit out of my territory since there was more than one sixth grade class. They all eyed me so unconcernedly I assumed that it was because to the "In" group, I was just the new kid on the block. I did not look to be the kind of addition they wanted to their group.

The other folk didn't seem to care one way or another. I was obviously not among the best dressed, nor was I one of the most outgoing kind of persons.

I kept telling myself as I looked at them, "They will not like me because I am not pretty and I can't afford those nice clothes." I was terrified to say the least.

Later that day I got the shock of my life. My teacher gave the class a math test. After lunch when we came back into the classroom she had graded the papers. She called me to her desk.

"Eddie, you have done remarkably well on your test even though this is your first day with us. I also took note of the report card you brought with you," she told to me. "I will be expecting great things from you, now."

"Thank you, Ma'am, I'll do my very best," I told her, then went back and took my seat.

When we were outside in the hall one of the nicest looking girls in the class and a couple of others came up to me. The girl spoke to me. "Hi, my name is Dorothy D, they call me Dee Dee. Can I ask you what the teacher was talking to you about? Did she get on you the very first Day?"

"No, I told her, "She complimented me for the grade I made on the math test we took earlier." I answered.

She looked at me kind of shocked then asked me, "You mean you mean you made a good grade on that test she gave us this morning?"

"Yes, I think that was an A on my paper she had on her desk. Why?"

"Because I have been here all year and, in her class all this time and I don't even think I made a passing grade, that's why!" She told me.

"So we have a smart girl in our class," Another girl said as they walked away.

I watched them kind of puzzled because I didn't know whether to take their remarks as compliments or wise cracks.

The next day Dee Dee came over to my desk and spoke to me right after the bell sounded.

"Good morning, Eddie, you remember me, I talked to you yesterday? She asked me. "We are glad to have you in our class."

To say I was surprised is putting it quite mildly. She was being nice to me even though I wasn't quite dressed to the standards of the rest of the class.

"She finally said, "Eddie I may as well tell you I am no good in arithmetic and since you seem to be so good at it, will you let me study with you? I don't live too far from your cousin, Annie Laura."

"I would be happy to study with you, if you want me to," I told her.

"Young lady, if you will please be seated, I think we get started with the class."

The teacher told Dee-Dee.

"Yes, Ma'am, I was only welcoming the new girl to our school and introducing myself and welcoming her to our school."

"Thank you, Dee Dee, now can we get on with the day?" The teacher told her.

The rest of that day and the weeks to follow were very nice. I even got to be part of the 'in' crowd because I was helping Dee Dee. I also joined a Spelling Bee the school had going on.

Things went this way for me and I was content and so were my sisters and brothers, but Mama thought the boys were becoming *too* independent, too soon. She also didn't like city life all that well on top of our having to pay rent, when we had a decent house to live in. She repeated this more often the longer we stayed. She also had the complaint that it was little much to have to keep up with so many children in the city.

Mama had a discussion with the children, at home with her one day about moving back home. We were all getting ready for the end of the school year anyway. We all thought it was ok. The two older boys where at Aunt Sis' when Zip got there and told them what we had decided. It was a real blow up when they came storming home that evening!

"Mama, what is this we hear about us going back home, and on day after tomorrow when school is out? Carlton asked in a voice showing he was not pleased.

Mama put up her hand stopping them, then and said, "Carlton you knew that we were only staying until I felt able to do things on my own. We've done that. I can do it as well I ever could. Besides it's too much trying to take care of a house full of children in a place like this. I have to pay rent when I have a house of my own sitting at home. There was no need for you boys to come tearing over here. We are going home!"

Carlton then said, "But, Mama we, me and Elouise, can help you better if you and all of us are here in the city. We can find jobs here can't we?"

"No, Carlton I don't see that. We have a farm and a home with what we need in it. It may not have all the conveniences that you have here, but it is ours. There won't be someone coming around every week to collect the rent because there won't be any."

"I won't have to sit home waiting until all times of the night for all my children to get home from jobs, and making the rounds of friends' houses, as well as worrying if all of them will make it back here alright! I don't know the city and what I do know is so different from what I am used to." Mama stressed as she talked to them.

"But, Mama, you can say all of that and then some, but you could get used to all of this if you stayed here a little while longer, Please!" Willie C argued.

"Now boys, I have talked it over with the other children and they seem to like the idea just fine. I know they will be leaving the nice friends they have made here but, since they don't mind why should you two make such a fuss?"

"But, Mama, we are all here together and we can see our cousins and Aunt Sis, Otis and Cotis and other members of the family more often. If we move back home it will be months before seeing all of them. Besides think of the money you'll have to spend just to get all of us back home." Carlton added.

They talked on and on at Mama, along with our cousin James who had tagged along with Carlton and Willie C, for what seemed like hours but she didn't change her mind one bit. She did ask us if we had changed our mind and want to stay in the city.

The rest of us knew how much she hated living in the city for so long and, most especially the idea of having to pay rent when we had almost new house of own at home. So, after arguing in vain for so long, my brothers and cousin finally gave up. We all got on with packing for our trip home.

The man Mama hired to take us home showed up on Saturday. And, we were at home by three o'clock that afternoon.

Family Back Home Again

After we got back home we found that there was furniture gone from the house along with a number of other problems that came at us all. We had to endure some very hard times again. Mama had to head up the family through things with rearing a family on her own that tried her patience, broke her heart and kept her with her prayer to God most avid and heartfelt. She admitted to needing the helper of us all/God, very badly in her prayers.

We had quite a few hardships to survive the next few years. Being a family on government assistance the size of our family made for tight budgeting and, then some. So, when the solicitors for itinerant farming came our way we had to head out. We would spin weeks at a time chopping cotton, pulling corn, picking cotton, gathering vegetables and the worst time I can remember was picking onions! (Not having the experience, one cannot imagine the repulsiveness of having an onion smell on you that you can't even wash off for days at a time!)

Most of the time we would have to go away during the working seasons, in order make ends meet for the rest of the year.

One time Elouise had a boyfriend who 'came a-courting' that I thought was really neat looking. His name was Tyrus. Well, this boyfriend came to see her one time, and brought his brother with him. He just happened to be just a little bit older than I was. Evelyn had her own boyfriend. She told me, to get dressed because he was going to have to talk to someone and it might as well be me. I was about

14 at the time and really eager for the chance. He turned out to be very handsome, with wavy hair, beautiful eyes and tall. I think I was "in love" before he had said two words to me!

"Hello." He said in the most beautiful voice I thought I had ever heard.

"Hi." I answered in what I hoped was my best voice.

"My name is Shelba and yours is Eddie." He said and smiled at me. I nearly passed out or swooned!

"How do you know my name?" I asked surprised.

"Why that is simple. You and my sister are classmates. She told me your name because I told her I was coming with Tyrus today, she knew Elouise. Besides Tyrus and Elouise have be courting a while and he told me a lot about you. I must say He didn't do you justice. You are much better looking than he could have described you."

This speech made me feel, on top of the world. He was just really trying to do what Mama had told us that males would do, when they wanted more than the words were saying. In other words he was selling me a bill of goods! My pausing, a minute made me snap out of my enthrallment.

My answer was, "Do you flatter all the girls you meet this way on the first meeting?"

"No, I don't find all girls I meet as captivating as you."

Not knowing what else to say to him after that flattering speech. I finally asked him, "Would you like to go out into the yard and sit out under the trees in the yard? It is probably cooler out there this time of the day."

"Why yes, it would be a lovely place to get to know you." He said almost hypnotizing me with those gorgeous eyes of his.

"You don't give a poor girl a chance, do you?"

"What do you mean; I don't give you a chance?" He retorted smiling at me, again.

"You know exactly what I mean Mr. Shelba Jordan. But, it is sweet of you to pretend you don't!"

Even though I was flattered, flabbergasted, **and** charmed to no end, Mama's warnings and, the romance novels I loved to read from the time I could, had let me in on a few things boys would say to a girl to make her do all they had in mind. I had the sense to keep it proper. But boy did it take effort, because in spite of that, I was really in love by the end of his visit!

When they left that evening, I went to Evelyn, "Evelyn, Tyrus brought his brother with him today and did you notice he is the most handsome thing you ever saw? He even told me I was beautiful, alluring and all kinds of nice stuff. Isn't it exciting?"

Evelyn's comments were, "Hold on a minute, Eddie you are falling too hard and what, you've only known him a day! Suppose he doesn't come back?"

"Oh he's coming back alright. He has to. I know he will, if he doesn't I'll just die!"

"For goodness sake Eddie, don't be silly. You act like you've lost your mind! Schh let me get away from you before I lose mine, too! What you have might be catching."

He continued coming over to see me, on Sunday evening, for more than a month before we even had the first kiss, then, WOW!

We courted for some time after that, Elouise and Tyrus broke up. Shelba stopped coming over as before. Then I saw him at 'happening' of some kind at the school.

Looking at the front of Butler Elementary-High School

Our community picnics were community wide celebrations or gatherings on the Butler School grounds because it was the largest place to have a gathering. On this particular occasion my brothers, my sisters and I went. While I was wandering around I happened to run into Shelba and we began talking. He seemed quite preoccupied with his hands or just uncomfortable in my presence all of a sudden.

"Hi," I said to him and he just smiled and looked at me. "Is there a problem?" I finally asked him.

He said nothing for a while then, I asked again. "Did I say or do the wrong thing just now? If so may we start again?"

"Eddie, uh... we are friends, huh?" He hesitantly asked.

"I thought we were, yes?"

"Well can we stay friends, no matter what? Can't we? He asked looking at me nervously.

"What do you mean, no matter what? Are you leaving or going away somewhere?" I questioned.

"Well, what I mean is that we get closer or we ought to not see each other anymore."

"What do you mean get closer? But, I thought we were close! You said you loved me. What happened, didn't you mean it?"

"Yeah, well, you, you...know... I mean real close? He answered.

"Do you mean what I think you mean?" I asked a bit indignantly "If you do, just don't even go there!"

"That's why I said we can just be friends," was his response.

I was floored. I just stood there. Tears came and he said, "Come here Eddie," as gave me his handkerchief, I went into his arms because I didn't want anyone else to see me crying. I held my head low while he said, Eddie we are young, we are going to meet others friends who will be the right person for us. It's just that... well we ought to call finish to our relationship as it is now."

With that last remark I handed him his handkerchief and walked away. I was too hurt to reply.

Mama had told us to be careful of boys who would make those kinds of offers but, I was also a romance reader who was convinced sex only came after marriage. I had no thought to it being any other way unless I wanted it to be if the fellow really loved me.

Sometime later Mama took the older children to west Texas and left the younger ones of us home who were still in school stayed at home with Aunt Georgia. It was during the cotton picking season during the fall, which was after school year had begun. She did it so she could pay the bills to make it through the winter and put away a little something.

After they had been gone for almost two months we received a letter from her telling us that Elouise was to get married to a man she had fallen in love with there. We were all happy for her but, real curious about what he looked like because we not met him.

Mama and the other children, Carlton and Willie C, stayed there until cotton had been almost picked then they came back home. Elouise and her husband came to meet us and stay for a little while. They couldn't stay too long because he had to get back and start work in the fields to prepare them for their winter crops. We thought he was a nice fellow the short while he was there. The only problem I had was that he was not long enough for me to get to know him. I would not be able to recognize should I see him again!

After that trip we got a car! To us, the car was a real sleek good looking white Mercury. Carlton had learned to drive and gotten his license and Willie C also knew how to drive. After we had the car awhile Mama asked Carlton to teach her how to drive it. She never reached real assurance or had time enough to obtain drivers license. Besides the folk in the community that Carlton talked to, were told that the car wasn't a family car it was, his own!

It served us well in getting us to the places that we had to go. It was crowded but we made it.

We didn't have it nearly long enough, before the day Willie C and George, a friend of his and Carlton's who was also and neighbor of ours, were on their way to or from Fairfield in the car when the unexpected happened. Willie C was driving down highway 84 and there was a dump truck stopped on the highway. Being young, cocky and not paying attention to what he was doing he didn't notice that the truck was completely stopped. He ran right into the back of it.

The car was smashed! Neither one of them was seriously hurt but, we were without a car, again. We had to rely on borrowed transport again, since we were not able to have the car repaired. It was the only car Mama ever bought. When it was gone she did not replace it. She also lost her courage and never tried to drive again in all the rest of her life.

Mama persevered in tending the land, and doing her best in taking care of us even though there was 30 acres less, of the land after Daddy died. Mama continued with the rearing of all of her children as best she knew how, in the nurture and admonition of the Lord. There were times when food was short. She I'm sure, wondered where the winter coats and clothes we needed all year long were going to come from, yet she always asked us to trust God to see us through. Her most recurring refrain to our complaints of not having whatever we needed or wanted was, "The Lord will provide!" Mama was still getting a bit of help from the check from the government.

There were times when we would be shelling some of the peas we had grown when Mama would resort to her propensity for drama by reciting some of her we remembered poetry to keep us focused on the job at hand rather than being so bored and resentful for all the work.

Georgia Mae remembers one in particular that she would break out with at the time we'd get whiney or bored with our lot as poor over worked creatures.

"Who's that coming up the path?

Run Betsy Jane and see,

I'll bet that's old Miss Perkins a' coming here for tea"

"Come in, Miss Perkin we're so glad you came

Please have a seat and stay awhile, thank you, Betsy Jane.

"Sit right down, and tell me all the news

It's been so awfully long I've almost got the blues."

You know, Mrs. Daisy got herself another new dress,

She's going to be surprised her money won't last, and she's going to be in a mess!"

Her presentation of the poems entertained us as we worked. They may have been the impetus for my tendency to enjoy putting together rhymes. They sometimes even come to me with the sound of music. I have a feeling hers did too. As I have stated before she did most things around the house to the tune of a song.

It's amazing that even though she had a lovely voice she never sang in the choir that

I know of, yet she would only lead a hymn or a song in the church.

Her love of the Lord she kept before us, since she continued to read her Bible aloud in our presence and not one of us can remember as long as she was in her own home did she forget or omit our Sunday morning prayer with the family.

Life Goes On

Though things happen in our lives
The kinds of things that may cause us pain
We just need to trust in God, who will give us the strength
To look up to Him, He will give us the power to start all over again
Mama found another husband, he was the younger brother
Of a man known communitywide as a pioneering man of vision
His entrance into our lives came
With what had to be, for him, a momentous decision.
You see he married a woman
With a number of children still at home to raise
One could speculate that he needed none at his age,
He probably thought himself through with that part of life's phase.
He was already the father of grown children
And even had grand children in his life
When he gets a whole new herd of them,
Since he was taking, my Mama, as his second wife.

Luke Durham

"Mr. Durham"

Meet "Uncle Luke" Mama's third husband whose background I got to know more of than I do of my own mother's **and** father's heritage! He was called by that name by most folks in the community. His name was well known even though he moved away from the area more than once before deciding to marry Mama. His father's and brother Rance's activities in the area made sure of that, even if he had not continued to frequent the area all his life as he did.

With Uncle Luke's help, and that of Robert, he has an interest in genealogy He was put on the trail for information after hearing a little of it, and he found out about their background history. Robert gathered lots of his fraternal background information about the family. But, just as in the Bible, the maternal side of his family seems to have been lost along the way.

Robert was able to trace the Durham family history all the way back to an African named Gobi! The records are not concrete but circumstances make us believe Gobi was purchased by a planter in South Carolina after getting Uncle Luke to give information on the close family members.

Wherever it was, Gobi, an African slave, became the father of Belton, Allen, Miner, Ike, Christopher and Anderson. Allen, Gobi's oldest son, Luke's Father was born in slavery. It is believed he was born somewhere around 1834. Circumstantial evidence indicates that Allen was owned by a planter named Robert Winfield Durham who lived and died in the Fairfield District of South Carolina. The time of Mr. Robert Durham's death, the records shows two dates, was either December 13, 1847 or February 18,

1848. During a war sometimes about then, the records were scrambled. The date of 1852 is in some of the records seems to be the date that may indicate when his widow and three of their sons moved to Louisiana taking their slaves with them.

It is believed that they moved to the area of Mansfield, in DeSoto Parish, Louisiana. All we do know for certain is that Louisiana was where Allen, Gobi's eldest sons lived. Allen was the person who was Luke Durham's father.

Shortly after the Emancipation Proclamation was signed, Allen Durham and his family moved to Texas because they are listed in the Freestone County Census for 1870. When Allen came to Texas he brought seven children with him: Rance, Wash, Taylor, Sylvia, Tethia, Johnny and Georgia. It is either ironic or intentional that being born in the Fairfield District of South Carolina that Allen brought his family to the area of Fairfield, Texas!

After arriving in Texas information of his first wife, Alice Mack was not mentioned so we *assumed* she had passed away. What we do know is that after coming to Texas, Allen met and married a woman named Hanna Wafer. He then became the father of six more children: Willie, Syrenia, Henry, Sammy, Richard and Luke. Luke Durham, Allen's baby child, was born November 27, 1888 to him, with his wife, Hanna Wafer Durham. He was the last of thirteen children born to Allen Durham. He had a very good memory when he talked me in the 70's about his earlier life, even at the age of 90 years he remembered some of the songs his mother sang as well as what one of her favorite dresses looked like! He liked to talk and I liked to listen.

He also remembered that when his mother died, his father took them to Elkhart and got someone there to take care of him and his sister, Syrena. However, he remembers staying there only a short while, then coming back to the Butler Community to stay with his daddy. Their home was in the area not too far from the "Crossroads," about a mile or so from highway 84 in the area near that is now Gaston's Temple.

The public school, for me as well as the children in the several communities around there, was built down the road from where his home had been. This community is between the small towns of Fairfield, Freestone County and Palestine, in Anderson County. This community is closer to Fairfield, where Allen Durham chose to live when he came from Louisiana to Texas.

The area is used by the community as a place for gatherings on holidays and special occasions. This is only about 3 miles or so from where my Daddy and his second wife, Mrs. Teasey bought, the property that became, for my family, home!

Uncle Luke's oldest brother Rance Durham became very well known throughout the area we all lived in. He owned lots of property there and was active in local politics. Rance was even selected as chairman of the Black Republican Party in Freestone County in the early 1900's.

Uncle Luke also remembered when his father, Allen Durham, took sick at their home and they were taken to live with his brother, Johnny where he died when Uncle Luke was only 12 years old. After his dad's death Uncle Luke lived for a time with his sister Sylvia and then his brother Henry.

Uncle Luke's Sister

When he was 28, in 1908, he walked from home to Palestine, 36 miles away, and got his first public job! There, he worked at the Round House for the railroad company and later several other places. He also worked in Teague, Texas. I'm sure he walked to Teague to get the job there, too. He continued to be a real walker to and from Fairfield and other places until his health failed. (For years he threatened to walk to Dallas on more than one occasion.)

Uncle Luke first married Molly Morgan from the Lone Star community which was not too far from his home in the Butler. The marriage produced five children: Classic, Sylvia, Corinne, Lela, and Carlton. They lived on, and farmed the land of a man named Carl Franklin for eighteen years.

He also worked for a man named Caleb Evans, by the day, for a time after all the children were grown and his wife died.

Uncle Luke then moved to Mart, Texas in McLennan County and worked for a man there whose family liked him so much the daughter even invited him to her birthday parties. He refused to go other than to take a plate of food.

Uncle Luke being the kind of man of he was and with his unusual wit, said he told her, "If you want a black monkey, you are going to have to go farther than me. I won't be your play monkey to entertain folks at your parties."

She must not have been angry because he only left the employment of this family after he married Mama.

Mama got to know Uncle Luke when he was visiting with his nephews Anderson Durham, the son of his oldest brother, Rance, and his Great nephew Walter (Nit) Durham. They lived at the Crossroads across the street from the grocery store. This was the meeting place for the communities of Lone Star, Bethel, Shiloh, Rabbit Ridge, and others communities and also where so many of them bought groceries. He must have gotten to know or made a connection with Mama there, because later he started coming over to our house for visits. They later became husband and wife.

Mama always addressed him as "Mr. Durham" then, and until her death. We addressed him as Uncle Luke then and continued to do so.

They married on December 18, 1951. At the time Mama was a widow with nine children at home! Uncle Luke's presence in Mama's and our lives could have reminded us of Daddy, especially since they were both at least 22 years older than mama and, he had a very dry witted sense of humor. He would smile but, didn't laugh out loud as much or as loud Daddy did.

He was a real addition to our household. Mama tried all she knew how to make him feel comfortable and not overwhelmed with all of us. She would let him eat at the table in the kitchen away from all of us during meals so he didn't have to deal with the bunch of us.

Luke Jr.

Mama got pregnant and gave birth to my baby brother Luke Durham, Jr. to make Mama the mother of her 14th child. He was the 13th she had given birth to, since the first one, Ausie, she and Daddy adopted. Junior, what we all called him, was the baby of the family.

He was born October 14 1952. He was a cute little rascal. He was just another brother to us that added to Mama's brood of children to love and care for. Uncle Luke was so pleased and proud.

Uncle Luke could make folk fall out laughing and he might just show a smile or two. Yet he could laugh and make others laugh with him. Mama was trying to teach me to cook and I made the biggest mess with what was supposed to be a cake. He was the only one who would eat any of it. He said it was unusual looking and the consistency very odd but, it tasted weirdly good. He took a couple of days to eat it. He wouldn't let me throw it away. In spite of telling me that he should tell whatever man I chose to marry that I could really make a sticky mess for, what I wanted to call, a cake!

While He was married to Mama he mostly just watched her attend church each Sunday at Shiloh for a while, then Mama began attending Owens Chapel Church of God in Christ in between times of the by monthly services at Shiloh Baptist Church. Uncle Luke did not attend church anywhere. He would make comment about Mama's church attendance. This did not deter Mama's faithfulness in attending either church. He would even give her a quarter to put in church a few times!

By this time I had gotten old enough to be in the choir and I taught a class for the Baptist Young People's Union (BYPU) and Sunday school. Along with being a member of the choir, I was also a soloist. I even remember singing one of the songs that Tennessee Ernie Ford made famous, "**Peace in the Valley**" quite often. Folk even asked me to do it and some others on funerals programs even at the other churches in the area.

Like most of the family, Mama sang, but only at home, there she was always singing a song as she worked and, to whoever was the baby. Like Mama, I also had a love of singing. I had no musical knowledge I had no idea of the keys I sang in. Sometimes I could sing in more than one voice or tone,

I learned to sing alto on some songs tenor on some and even soprano a musician told me. It depended on the song being sung. I just loved to sing and still do.

One man, who accompanied me, on the piano as I sang for a funeral, got really upset with me when I began singing in a key that was different from the one he was playing! The melody I could keep up with and I didn't notice, especially since I was at that time upset because dead person was someone I cared for. I never attempted to change keys. He commented on it afterwards, but not to me. He complained to another person and someone else heard and asked me about it. I was really embarrassed.

There was an incident that happened at the Shiloh Baptist Church where we attended that I really got called on by my stepfather. The Deacons were the leaders of different Tribes/ small groups for the church on the pastoral days or special occasions. They had certain members of the congregation assigned with them to generate money for the church or its activities. Mama and her family was part of Deacon Lee T's Tribe. "Cousin Lee T" is what we called him. Well, it was on one of these special times after Mama married Uncle Luke that Cousin Lee T was calling the names of his contributors and he called, Everlena Durham, Eddie Durham…. I went, in my mind, whoa, I'm no Durham!

After we went home I made sure I told Uncle Luke about it. Then I had the audacity to tell him. "I am not a Durham, and I wouldn't be a Durham!" He laughed at me and teased me about it. "You don't have to be young lady." (This comment was going to come back and bite me.)

Mama decided to join Owen Chapel Church of God in Christ sometime later. My younger sisters chose to join at Owens Chapel, too after they were old enough to join the church as well. In our house at that time you didn't join until you were twelve or very near. I never did join there, officially, though I attended with everyone else, I remained a member at Shiloh Baptist Church.

Uncle Luke was **very** frugal we had, most of the time, but Mama didn't seem to mind. His behavior could become cold at times, too. Yet she continued to be the kind of submissive wife the Bible stated a woman should be. He was receiving a check each month, I have no idea what the amount was but, it didn't make any difference since he didn't do much sharing with us or Mama and very little with Junior.

The only money Mama got was the money we made working on the farm and on our trips to do itinerant farm work; picking cabbage, cotton chopping and picking cotton somewhere and on one occasion we even harvested some awfully stinky onions. Every once in a while Uncle Luke would give her a dollar or two. In spite of this side of him he was, to the family someone who could to bring lots of laughter to the family and a smile to Mama's face.

Growing Into Adulthood

Even though I was not at what many would call the right dating age, I somehow managed to have a boyfriend or two by this time. Some of the only things that kept me chaste were Mama's teachings. She told me that anything done that you did not want anyone to know about most likely was either wrong, or shameful and shouldn't be done. This was one of the ways she talked about having sex before one was suppose to. She never really came out and talked frankly about it.

My constant reading of everything I could, including, romance novels also gave me views of what could go on in relationships, too. Reading about things in those books really was enlightening about sex as well giving me a way to handle some situations.

My first really serious relationship after the Shelba fiasco was with a very nice looking young man named Benard. He was a very honorable young man as well. We had a very enjoyable relationship. He gave me his class ring wear right after he got it. I think I wore it more than he did for the first couple of years.

Benard followed the kind of script that Mama taught me and the things I had learned from the books I loved to read was what a gentleman was to do. He was always such a gentleman and what I thought a 'steady' was supposed be if he respected the girl he was involved with.

Later when he decided to move on, he even ended our courtship in a very gentlemanly fashion. I do believed, since time has passed, that he fell in love with the woman that is his present wife, and found a way to let me down easy. All I can say is that he still has my respect for being so gentle with me.

My First Job

The summer of 1955 I made the decision, with the permission of Mama, to go to Dallas with my sister Elouise.

While I was there I got my first job working, as a dish washer. The first dish washing job that I got was a little too much, I did not keep it. It was as a dish washer at Luby's Cafeteria. I lasted for just a half day! I got started that morning but the task took everything out of me, I nearly passed out it was so hot there. When I went for my lunch break and felt I could not take it anymore so, I didn't go back.

Later that week I got another job at the Dallas Club, it was as a dish washer, too. I felt it was one I could handle. It was in one of the tallest buildings in downtown Dallas. I enjoyed it, It gave me my first paycheck, since I never went back to get anything from the first one.

When I went to Dallas I had planned on staying the entire time with my sister Elouise. I only remained for a few weeks with her. One night she and I had a difference of opinion on what should be done, I decided I was going to move in with my brother Cotis, his wife Arletha, and their son. Our difference was such we were not able to fix and, with both our mind sets, it wasn't going to be. This happened in the middle or the night but, in the state I was in, I left right then.

My staying with Cotis was such that it made for a very rewarding summer experience for me. While I was there my brothers Cotis and Willie C all started to sing in a group (a Quartet called the "Crowns of Glory") they practiced at Cotis' house. I loved it. While they were rehearsing they decided I would join the group for the time I was in town. I even got to go around to many churches in the area and a few out of town.

Walter "Nit" Durham

While I was there in Dallas I got to have the experience of seeing my first scary movie it was called **_Doctor Jekyll and Mister Hyde._** I went to the movie alone and it took me days before I could sleep the night through. I have never gotten over my dislike for scary movies since!

At the end of August I went back home to enroll in school again. When I did go home I had a life changing experience. It came in the form of a tall young man. His name was Bobby Jean Durham.

Uncle Luke's grand nephew, Walter "Nit" Durham, had a son that I became entranced with him and began thinking he was THE one!

I have thought about our getting together along with how it all got started. Then I remembered that it probably started with a visit or two he and his father made to 'see his Uncle Luke.' Bobby, was then in college at Prairie View A & M College, but he was home during the summer of 1955. He had a job not too far from home. He was still there when I came home from Dallas. We would talk while Nit and he was there visiting Uncle Luke and when we went to the store at

Bobby Jean Durham

the Crossroad to get groceries or coming from town or another part of the area. Their home was sort of the meeting place for people in the community.

Bobby and Eddie in wedding attire

I Got Married

During this time we started "courting." In today's language we started 'seeing each other.' He came by the house to see me. His excuse to his family for coming over for a while, was that he was going to see his Uncle Luke.

This all happened before Bobby went back to college for the fall session. We became quite enamored of by each other. He went on back to school at P. V. when it began and I went back to Butler High School just as I had all the other times after a holiday.

When he went back to Prairie View we kept in touch with each other. We wrote letters to each other, often. He continued working after getting back to campus. He was soon able to buy himself a car! It was a yellow and white '52 Ford.

Bobby with his new car

Even with paying his own way through college he was able to afford it because of his hard work. He was also able to come home more often.

By this time he was a junior there at Prairie View and I was in eleventh grade in high at Butler High School.

By the beginning of the year of 1956 he had also decided that he was in love with me.

When young people get that first idea of marriage in mind, in those times, they thought all they needed, was to be in love, to live 'happily ever after.' He asked me to marry him!

But, experience teaches one that a lot more is necessary and we had to learn that through experience. Mama, was one who knew this quite well, and had a talk with the both of us when Bobby proposed the idea to her of our getting married. He persuaded her that it was really something we could handle **and** stay in school until we both graduated. She said if we thought we could do it she would not stop us. We became officially engaged on that Sunday, March 4, 1956.

I was ecstatic, and I think, so was Bobby. We had Mama's permission to get married. We set the wedding for the first Sunday, Easter Sunday, evening. It was during his spring holiday from college and everyone was off at that time. It was to be at 7:00 P.M. on April 1, 1956. Rev. L.C. McIlveen, the pastor of Shiloh Baptist Church, where I belonged agreed to do the ceremony for us.

One other thing I was ignorant about was preparing for the wedding. All knew was that I needed was a dress and a place to have the wedding. Somehow, Mama and I completed a quilt that she said I was supposed to have at the time I got married and even make my wedding dress as well.

We had the help of a few of the neighbors, and my sister Lula in making the quilt. My sister thought that I ought to use one of her daughters' dresses, since our money was very limited. I wouldn't accept that.

As a way of making extra money and help out with some the expenses, I learned to do hair. I had been doing my sisters' hair and mine. Afterwards, I don't know when, I started doing hair for a few other people in the community. I was doing that, just before my wedding because more of my customers were coming to get their hair done because this was Easter time.

Since it was a special time I had the patronage of several girls and women from the community. The weekend of my wedding, I was in the midst of more customers than usual because it was the Easter weekend. It was also the weekend for my wedding!

Bobby came over to see me on that Saturday. I was in the middle of doing a lady's hair. **He,** decided that I had to stop right then. He told me and the lady, "I do not want my bride to be tired on her wedding day."

So, he took the lady to my niece's beauty salon in his car. He told my niece why the woman's hair was half done. She was to pay her and not me for the hair-do. My niece was so sweet, and told him she was glad to oblige and finish the lady's hair.

My wedding was the very next day, since this was a Saturday. We spent the day relaxing and driving around. He then took me back home and told me to rest and he would see me the next morning.

He came back over at about ten the next day, my brother, Zip told him I had gone to

Dallas and was not there, as an April fool's joke. He came on in anyway and we spent most of the day together.

That evening at the wedding, one of our neighbor's Willie Estene Gibson was my maid of honor and Jodie Turner, Jr., one of Bobby's classmate and friend, was best man. Little Patricia Mims, the daughter of Tiny Mims a distant cousin, was the flower girl.

What I did not know at the time of our marriage was that my future mother-in-law was not convinced we should have been getting married. She and her mother were so totally opposed to our union. She felt so bad about it that she watched the wedding from their vehicle. She did not even get out during the whole time of the wedding!

My father-in-law and mother-in-law
Walter and Ovena Durham

It was performed on the front porch of my home. She was able to see everything from their pickup truck! She was upset to the point of anger yet, I never noticed anything out of the ordinary. I think I was just into the wedding and so happy at the time.

Mrs. Ovenia Durham, 'Sis', as we called her, was so afraid that Bobby would be forced drop out of college after he married me. I had no idea she felt that way because she treated me so lovingly at all times! Later on she even allowed me a few privileges she didn't allow her own daughters! She was always a very sweet loving mother-in-law! By the time she passed away I felt like an integral pat of the family.

She felt we should have waited until we both finished school. I had nothing that I could bring to the union except my love for her son. I was still in high school, he was in college. With nothing and very job experience. They, as parents, were doing all they could. He had seven other children that had to be cared for and educated. He was the oldest, and she may have been expecting his help to educate their other children after he graduated and got a decent job. The only thing like encouragement Bobby received to go on and marry me came from his father. His comment was, "Do you think you can do this and keep up you schooling? You, better than anyone else know your situation."

Bobby told him he felt he could handle it. His Dad's only comment was, "Go for it, then."

After the wedding when the school break was over, Bobby went back to Prairie View and I stayed with Mama and went back to high school at Butler. When I got back to school I was called into the principal's office where he told me he had heard that I had gotten married. I admitted it and he asked what I planned to do. I told him that I didn't plan to drop out of school, I was going to go on and finish so I could go to college.

He was quite surprised that I intended to continue school. He told me he had never known it to happen before that he knew of, but, he didn't know of anything being illegal about it. He wished me luck and sent me back to class. Even though a few of the teachers asked me about my being married and, in school as well, everything else continued as usual.

With Mama's support and advice when I went to her for answers, we made it through the rest of the year. Bobby worked that summer as he had done since going to college only we were together. We separated again in September at the beginning of the school year for 1956-57.

I was on the track and field team and a member of the varsity basketball team. I continued to be, even though I was questioned extensively by the coach I was allowed to continue. Things continued this way for two months. I even got to play in several basketball games. By this time, we decided this was not what we wanted.

We then decided we should live together. We told his parents and Mama about it. Mama, and I think, his parents thought that it was workable idea.

He found us a place in Hempstead, Texas, a town near the college campus. I enrolled at Sam Schwartz High School which was up the street from the little house we lived in.

This is when the real work of our marriage began, during my last year in high school. Bobby drove everyday to classes on campus at Prairie View. I walked up the street. This continued until the last semester when Bobby was at the point in his program when he needed to do his student teaching. At this time he was accepted also at Sam Schwartz High School to do his student teaching of civics there as the wife of the principal's student, that meant he was my civics teacher!

The first six months of our marriage had been no real strain for either of us because I lived with Mama to complete school for that for that year. We saw each other only on weekends and holidays. Our living together is when the real struggle to make a marriage began.

We had to really struggle to keep our heads above water. Bobby had to work on campus each night. I did what I could to help but it was very little since I had no skill that was marketable and since I had had only one job before, beside field work and, I was in school as well. However working together we made the year. I finished high school there at the Sam Schwartz High School while he finished up his bachelor degree at Prairie View A&M College, too.

Me graduating from **high school**

Bobby graduating from college

Things went fairly smoothly for the next two years because after Bobby had gotten his Bachelors Degree he became Director of Student Activities at the college while I began my college attendance. We were still not prosperous but we were still not starving either. We were staying in an apartment building in Prairie View, Texas, close to the campus that belonged to one of the college professors. The building housed the Greyhound Bus Station and since our apartment was right next door we agreed to run that station. That was to be my job. The schedule of buses was such that I could do it in between classes.

It was during my first year as a student at Prairie View that I got pregnant and lost my first child. It hurt us both badly! We had hoped not to have children so early but, had not tried very hard not to. When I found I was pregnant we were both happy in spite of everything. We thought we'd manage. Then during the fourth month I lost the baby.

For a while it seemed like everything changed, we quarreled the Sunday after I had been released from the hospital about a week. It was an awful fight. It started over my visiting our neighbor's house. We had had fights before but it had never gotten heated as it did this time. He struck me!

For days afterwards we were both quite cool to each other. I also talked with Mama about praying with me, without telling her what the problem was, she did. Then I decided that he was just taking out his hurt over our loosing the baby. His worry about our financial condition and his hope for us to succeed that caused him to blow up. I finally asked him if that was how he felt and he reluctantly admitted as much.

Getting out of the car after class, at out apartment next door to the Greyhound Bus Station

During my sophomore year we faced the first real big crisis in our marriage. I had just lost our second baby when I noticed that Bobby was acting quite differently. Again he was crankier harder to please and sometimes downright cold toward me. I said nothing hoping I was just imagining things. Then one day I was working in the Bus Station when I saw a letter on the floor near the counter. It was addressed to Bobby!

It was written by a woman from a small town not too far from where we lived since it was already open I took it out and read it and got the shock of my life. It was a 'love' letter to my husband!

When I finished reading it my heart felt as if it had been torn from my body. From the contents it was someone he had been seeing. It didn't say for how long but, he had been seeing her, slept with her!

I walked around in a daze for what seemed like hours. Then I decided to go confront him in his office because I couldn't wait until he returned to the house to ask him about it. I walked into his office; he sat at his desk and I stood across from him and threw the letter across it at him.

"Bobby I found this letter this morning! Is what it says true? Have you been seeing this woman?" I asked.

He just looked at the letter. "I love you; I don't know why I did this. I saw her and it just happened. Please, Marie, don't look at me like that!"

I had been hoping that there had been some kind of mistake but, he just admitted to the whole thing.

"Why? How could you see her, if you really love me? Why, Bobby, why......?"

His response was, "I do still love you as much as ever. I don't know why I have been seeing her. Really I don't! Please, believe me!"

I just got up and left his office. I drove around for hours crying and thinking.

Then I drove to her address to see the woman. I talked to her but; it didn't help make me feel any better.

I thought about leaving him after I left his office. When I got back to the apartment, he was there and we talked most of the night. He tried to tell me our marriage was worth saving. I was still not sure he meant it. Even if he did, I was so hurt I couldn't believe a thing he said!

The next day after he left for work, I packed, made myself a ticket and caught the bus home to Butler!

When I got to the bus stop in front of Bobby's parent's home I got out, walked right by on the way to my home without even stopping. I walked carrying my bag the five or so miles to get to Mama's.

Mama wanted to know why I was home by myself in the middle of the week. I didn't ever tell her outright what had happened. I felt kind of ashamed somehow I felt it had said I wasn't good enough. I couldn't get another reason that it wasn't. I felt so deep and hurt it was somehow partly, my fault. I also didn't want to upset Mama with my problems. She had always handled her own problems with the help of God.

Even though she didn't know why I had come she knew something was wrong. She just prayed for me and let me know she would do what she could to support me. Yet, she would only say of my husband that he was a good man.

She did however point out to me that she had tried to tell us that everything was not going to be to our liking but we said we'd be able to handle hard times, but she would be there for me

Bobby came home that weekend. We talked and he convinced me that our marriage really was worth saving and by then I was more amiable to listening. I had missed him while I had been gone, so, I went back to Prairie View that Sunday.

We seemed to develop a stronger marriage after that. Oh, things weren't rosy all the time and I had a few trust issues but it got better as time went on.

While we were all visiting at home together for a holiday or some other reason, Elouise had the idea that it would be nice to have a family reunion! We all talked about it and decided to make an effort to help her get it together. We decided that all of Mama's **and** Daddy's children were to be invited to the gatherings at home. Uncle Luke was a real addition to the mix especially since he was a vital part of the family.

Many of our older sister Cardelia's children came each time we had it there. Sister Lula came alone sometimes and only some of Sister Edie's group ever showed up, on a very few occasions.

Kenneth Was Born

When I completed my junior year at the college I found I was pregnant again. Right after that time Bobby was taken by one of the professor's, a Mrs. Preston, to Port Arthur, Texas to apply for a teaching positions there. She told him it was one of the better districts in the state of Texas.

After he went, he had to take a test similar to the TCAT later, taken by all Texas teachers. He must have passed for he was hired by the Port Arthur Independent School District. He became one of the sixth grade teachers at Carver Elementary School where the principal was Miss Dorothy. She was also the owner of several apartment buildings. Bobby decided to take the one up over a garage at 810 San Antonio Avenue.

We also decided it would be best for me to go with him to Port Arthur, and come back to college after the baby was born. We were so happy he was starting this new job and we were having a baby, we moved.

I was on cloud nine the whole time. When we got settled I got the phone book and did the "eenney-meenny-miney-moe" thing to pick a doctor. Since we were new to the area and had no idea what doctor to see, or anyone we knew well enough to ask. I was blessed because I selected a very good one as it turned out! He was Dr. J. D. who became our family doctor as well, until he retired years later. I followed his orders very carefully.

Bobby's grandmother, Rebecca Simmons agreed to come and stay with me the last month of my pregnancy. While she stayed with us those few weeks just before the baby was born. I got to know and love her dearly. She was such a sweet lady and so very good to me.

Bobby took her home the first of March. He left me there, since they didn't think that I needed to be traveling so close to my delivery date. That week end, it snowed in Port Arthur! I was going down the stairs from our apartment and fell on my "sit-down" while he was gone. I was not hurt, thank God!

Grandmother Rebecca

Simmons Mama

When he returned he brought Mama back with him. She came to stay, help me get into the groove of caring for a child.

Our baby boy was born on March 8, 1960. It was a beautiful healthy baby boy that we named Kenneth Wayne. He was a darling and quite handsome, if I do say so myself! We were both so happy. Mama stayed awhile and helped to get me into the way of taking care of a small child.

This was the time I got to know what being a mother was-all about. I had a very memorable time of it. I found out where I wouldn't necessarily speak up for myself I would when it came to my baby!

Bobby had decided that he didn't need a new outfit for Easter. I thought he did. I **walked** downtown from our apartment carrying him many blocks to shop for his new Easter outfit. When he came home I dared him to say anything about it by just ignoring him.

Kenneth Wayne at five month in Denver, Colorado

When he was five months old we made our first trip to Denver, Colorado. Bobby was attending the University or Denver there as a part of what teachers in Port Arthur was supposed to do. He had decided that he would go alone. I planned to stay with my sister and his in Dallas while he was away.

It was an unpleasant experience for both of us. The baby and I being so far away from Bobby, we decided, it was too much. We missed each other terribly so after a short time we decide Kenneth and I should come out to Denver with him. That gave us our first passenger train ride and it was a lovely experience!

We got there and he and I were so happy to be together again. I got to meet his very nice Aunt Katie Mae and Uncle Henry when I first got there because we were staying with them. But, I also met his uncle Yale and his wife, his Aunt Claire and Uncle Prince who were there too. Uncle Yale lived in the city but Aunt

Claire and Uncle Prince lived at home in Fairfield, Texas, but were visiting up there for a while with Aunt Katie Mae and Uncle Yale and their spouses. Uncle Prince and Uncle Henry had a few qualities alike.

While he attended class, and Uncle Henry went to work, Aunt Katie Mae Tatum and I went on tours of the city and areas surrounding it. She took us to see the capital and many other sites around the city. Bobby got to see much of what I saw when he got out of class. We got to even go to Colorado Springs, where the U.S. Air Force Academy is, as well as so many other interesting sights in that area. One awe inspiring scene was the real high road that thank God, we didn't go on. They said that from it things/ cars on the lower place below looked like toys! No, not for me!

Uncle Henry and Aunt Katie Mae Tatum

Me, Aunt Claire, Aunt Katie and neighbor's child

When we returned home after the summer, we decided that I would go back to Prairie View so that I could get my Bachelor of Education Degree. Even though it meant I would be there with the baby alone, and we would be separated for nine whole months. I did.

Having a baby with me in college didn't prove to be much of a problem for me. I roomed off campus, and walked to and from classes each day. It helped me to keep my tasks in focus. It was a bit hard at times walking in the rain and cold to and from classes sometimes, especially when I had inadequate clothing for bad weather, and taking care of a rambunctious child I even had to take him to class with me sometimes, **and** while studying. But, I made it! My teachers were very nice because I could usually keep him quiet during class, amazingly, none of them ever complained! They would just tell me he was cute. Not one told me I couldn't bring him into the classroom.

I finally made the school year all the way to May, 1960 but, I had to go the summer term to complete everything I needed to meet the degree requirements. Bobby decided to attend the summer session too, because the P.A.I.S.D. encouraged their teachers to go back often, they even paid their tuition every two years when they did.

It was a pretty rugged time with us since Bobby was not much of a hand at taking care of a small baby. He was afraid he would drop him or something. a few other problems popped up again, too. I talked with a priest. I didn't get much help from him.

It was then I decided I had to be my own person. Up to this time I was trying to emulate Mama and be the quiet submissive little wife. I figured I, had to make a few changes. I was determined the marriage was going to work if I could make it by my own efforts. I couldn't just leave. By August I had completed everything and to get my degree. I graduated in spite of a pretty heavy heart much of the summer.

Once I had graduated from Prairie View I returned home. I decided I was not going to let him, or anybody else ruin MY marriage I felt I had too much tied up in it. I still loved him in spite of everything. I planned to do all I could keep our home together. I felt that if I could still love him he must be worth something.

I began doing special little things for him that I knew he liked. I cooked his favorite meals; I dressed up for his arrival home each evening from school. I would compliment him often as I could. Never once did I nag or complain nor ask question him about where he had been, or had been doing. I kept this up for more than a week before he even seemed to notice! It was a difficult time because I longed to have some answers. But, it finally began paying off. He began being nicer. He was away less often until finally he was not going out any at all without telling me, mentioning where he was going.

I had not gotten hired when I graduated, but later in September I was hired in Orange, Texas at an elementary school to teach third grade there. I had to drive across the Rainbow Bridge. For everybody else it seemed to be no big deal but, for me, it was an experience since I had realized I was so afraid of heights. That bridge was one of the highest I knew of in Texas or any other state. I had to cross it twice every week at least. Thank God, I only had to work there one semester. The Lord blessed and I was to be able to take over the job of a lady who was going on maternity leave. She was teaching third grade, in Port Arthur at Lamar Elementary School.

It was a few months after I was added to the Port Arthur Schools that we decided we were able to build our own home. It was built on a piece of property that that Bobby had purchased sometime earlier. We visited some sample homes in the area found one we liked and could afford, in Beaumont and decided to have it built. It was completed and we were able to move into it in the fall of 1962.

Our first Home, built in 1962

At this time Kenneth was being taken care of by a very nice baby sitter. However, within a few months we enrolled him into the Rebecca Martin Nursery School. He attended there for several years. While there, he was part of many very nice activities. Some of them the mothers were involved in as well. I remember one program where both the children and the mothers were taking part in where we were all dressed in black and white.

I was on the program. I went up to do my part, I completed my activity and was going back to my seat when I noticed my shirt was falling off. I had to thank God that my undergarment and the outfit were a white top and black bottom, too. My black skirt fell almost all the way down to the floor before I realized it had come loose, and no one there seemed to notice what had happened. They all seemed surprised when I talked about it. I was so relieved that they hadn't

Kenneth made some very good friends while attending the nursery school. We thought it was a very worthwhile experience for him.

Ceremony for the Rebecca Martin Nursery School with the mothers Ken is in the front row the fourth child from the right.

Bobby decided to go back to Denver again when he was scheduled to go back to get more college hours. When we were preparing to go on this trip, we planned see the country as we traveled in the car as he had done before. Bobby's grandmother, Mrs. Rebecca Simmons decided she would go with us! She said she would have a chance to visit relatives there for a while. She seemed to have had a lovely time.

We didn't just sit around while we were there this time either because we visited sights we'd only heard about before.

(Aunt Katie Mae, Kenneth and me and Kenneth and Bobby outside the mint)

We got to travel to the Denver Mint and many other places in Colorado while we were there. At the mint we had a chance to go in and while there looked at the way coins were formed and printed. They even had open big bins/tubs of incomplete coins that we could run our hand or hands through. They didn't worry about our taking any of them because they were not printed yet.

We went into the mountains, to places where people were panning for gold! I even tried it out to see what it was like. There were a lot of other folks doing it too. I didn't get anything. We went into some old mines. The temperature in the middle of the summer and it was about 52 degrees inside.

It was on the trip we made to the Cave of the Winds that I learned that how bad my fear of heights could limit my enjoyment of sightseeing. I went outside to look down at the hairpin curve we had had to travel to get up to the cave's entrance, I nearly fainted. I had to go back inside and catch my breath. I also went to Seven Falls and even got dizzy just looking up at an old covered wagon on the top of the falls, so I had no thought of climbing them even though my husband teased me about it.

At the beginning of the next school year we, Bobby and I went back to Prairie View to work on getting our Masters of Education Degrees. Our going each Saturday during the school years and spending summers on campus made it possible to get our degrees earlier. We went with our very active little son, who at about 6 had the gall to refer to me with some girls he liked to hang out with on campus while we were in class as "His old Lady." I pretended I didn't hear him the day I heard him myself, and kept walking.

When we had completed the requirements, which we did by the summer of 1966, both our mothers came down and were there to watch us receive our degrees, together along with our son Kenneth.

Bobby and me at graduation

Bobby, Sis, Mama, Me, and Kenneth

During that school year I made another decision that will affect me for life I always believe for the better. I joined the Delta Sigma Theta Sorority along with four other ladies who became very dear sisters. We all made it!

We went through a few experiences that drew us close during that time but, we were never treated the way so many others that I have heard about happening to so many other fraternal orders had put pledgees through. (It is still a sorority that is above the all the rest!)

Ladies who became Deltas with me; Cole, Wheatfall, me, Peters and Pierre

Our Trip to California

The next summer after our graduation we decided to take a long trip. This time we hoped to travel from home to Denver and then across the states of Colorado, Utah and Nevada, to Los Angeles, California and visit there.

On this planned trip we decided to see if our mothers would like to go with us. Wow, were we surprised when they were both excitedly said they would go!

We were all preparing to go, getting their clothes together and all the stuff we would need another issue came up that really shocked us. It was about my stepfather.

We always knew Uncle Luke was a very frugal person, and sometimes we actually said he was stingy but, this trip proved how frugal he really could be. Mama talked to Uncle Luke as we were about to leave. He was ok with her taking the trip with us. He gave us all instructions about being careful and that we should send him a postcard or a letter along the way. He then handed Mama one **quarter** to take with her!

"Only a quarter, Uncle Luke, is that all she gets?" I asked him.

"What will she need more for? Aren't ya'll going to carry her? Won't ya'll be taking care of her while she is gone?" Uncle Luke asked me.

"Yes, we are going to take care of her, but won't she want some money of her own to have?" I asked.

His question was, "What for?"

I just gave up, and threw up my hands, and he just laughed!

On the way, I noticed that when we stopped at places to eat Mama would always only order a hamburger. I wondered why she never selected anything else.

Our break for the first part of the trip was in Amarillo, Texas. We stayed there for the night. Mama and Sis shared a room at the motel on the first leg of our trip to Denver and each hotel we stopped at on the trip. All of us had a wonderful time during the drive to Denver.

Mama, Sis, and Kenneth enjoyed the sights along the way as well as the increase in altitude. I was alright except when the roadway dropped away on one side or the other and then my phobia would drive my breath away.

**We had our first look at mountains up close and personal.
Ken even got a chance to play a bit in snow in the summer!**

After getting there to Denver we visited with relatives of Bobby and Sis. We stayed for awhile had fun then, continued our trip continued our trip through the mountains. We stopped along the way where we got to see snow in the middle of summer!

I got to see that Mama and Sis were in much better physical shape than I was. They out walked me over and over again! I would have to stop and rest they almost kept up with Kenneth even while we were on the mountaintop.

As we were passing through Las Vegas we got to see what gambling **everywhere** we went was like! It was in the diners, the hotels, the service stations and every other public place you went even some restrooms.

Kenneth and his daddy went into a fast food place and Kenneth dropped a quarter on the floor; a woman was at one of the slot machines, she saw the quarter Kenneth dropped picked up **his** quarter, dropped it into the slot machine she was playing just like it was hers. She paid no attention to the child's yelling about her taking his money! She just offered a choice word or two about missing the prize she hoped to get and walked out the door!

After that we just stopped a few times to take a few pictures along the strip, and admire the beautiful structures along the way. One visiting there now would have no idea how different the sights are today. I have been there since then and the place was a complete shock in how much it has changed since the way it was back then.

I had my picture taken on 'The Stripe' in Las Vegas as it looked in the 1960's

By this time I had mentioned Mama's choice of a hamburger at every food stop no matter where. I then suggested she might like to try something else. She finally let us order chicken for her. When it came it was not cooked properly! There was blood near the bone. After that I kept my opinion to myself.

While we were in Los Angeles, California Bobby's cousin Archie Durham took us to a restaurant, Bobby and I ordered steak cooked medium rare. Sis decided to order the same as what we asked for. Mama ordered her usual hamburger. We thought Sis was ok with it.

Later on that evening when we were going to bed I heard Sis telling Mama, "Miss Babe do you know that the meat we got was not even done! I ate what I could just like it was ok but, I certainly could have eaten some plain food!"

That's when Mama told her, "Now you know why I usually order a hamburger. I know what I am getting. These children can eat some unusual things now days!"

As I said before, I learned that both Mama and Sis were much more in shape for walking and seeing things than I was on that trip. They went off and left me on more than one occasion. They both had a wonderful time.

Bobby, Kenneth and I got to take a tour of the sets of *"Daktari'* and *"Cowboy in Africa"* with one of Bobby's cousins and my former classmate, Hobart Durham. He worked there as a part of the casts on the two shows while he lived in California. This tour was very exciting for us since these were two very popular television shows at that time.

Hobart Durham

Chuck Connors and Kenneth on the set of *Daktari*

We even got to see our first Hummer vehicle. It was being used on the set by Chuck Connors. Kenneth got to play with the apes from the set of *"Daktari"* and was entertained by one guy from *"Cowboy in Africa."* He even got to ride in the Hummer.

The Sunday we were there Mama went to spend a little time with my sister, Evelyn, her husband, Elbert Rider and her daughter Carolyn. Sis, Bobby, Kenneth and I went to church with Cousin Archie.

Bobby, Kenneth, Sis and Me dressed to go to church
Standing outside Cousin Archie Durham's home in Los Angles

On the way back from California we traveled through the states of Arizona and New Mexico back to Texas. What a trip it turned out to be! The scenes were splendid but the temperature in Arizona was the hottest I have ever experienced. I had heard about it but, we were there, to experience it! While traveling through Arizona we got to feel the hottest weather we had ever been in. It felt as if the air conditioner in the car was not working at times. I got up to at least 120 degrees!

When we returned Uncle Luke was visibly glad to see Mama and all of us when we returned. It couldn't help but remind him that for the whole trip he only gave her a quarter for the entire trip!

For years after, we remembered what Uncle Luke gave Mama to take with her on that trip. He could be entertaining and lots of fun. He was especially nice when we would gather for our usual family gatherings. All those who were able to come were there, for us to visit with, eat, then visit together some more and eat some more! All the family members got to know Uncle better. He also seemed to enjoy it all as much as we did.

I got sick a year or so after our trip and I realized what a good decision I made to stay with my husband in spite of the problems we were having earlier in our marriage. He was really there for me throughout the whole ordeal. He was caring for me alone along with our son not once did he complain about the task even though I knew at times he was stressed. Even when I went back to work he did everything he could to make things easier for me.

We Traveled to Mexico

In the summer of 1968 Bobby and I were inspired to take another trip during our summer time off. This time we went to Mexico! We liked traveling by car, this meant we could go as far as we liked and at the pace we wanted to travel. It was we felt, more rewarding to go at our own pace.

We got to see the city of San Antonio for the first time. While we were there we visited spots of interest around the city.

Scenes at and around San Jose`

We spent a good while seeing what San Antonio had to offer. We had heard so much about some of the Missions. I even taught a unit about them to my third grade class. I was fascinated looking at them. We went to visit all of them while we were there. While we were at the San Jose Mission they did a service. I didn't know before that, that any of them were used anymore for anything other than looking at.

I was especially surprised about the Alamo. I had heard so much about the Alamo and knew about how historical it was. I thought it would be way off by itself but it was right in the middle of downtown!

We enjoyed our stay there anyway and got to see lots of things in that interesting city. Our journey continued to be eventful as we continued southward to border to Laredo, Texas. We stayed at the Ramada there and ate at their coffee shop there.

Bobby and Kenneth at the Alamo and outside the Ramada at Laredo, Texas

We had the experience of dealing with border patrol as we went to go across. There we learned that some of the crossing guards liked to have their "palms greased" before doing their job. My husband was not the kind to condone that kind of behavior. One of the more valid reasons was that we didn't have the extra cash for that kind of thing. We sat in the waiting area for little time before being allowed to cross the border.

After crossing the border into Mexico we had the experience of seeing how many of the people of Mexico lived. I also realized that their conditions were much worse than many of us had ever had to live in. We chose to stay in Monterrey, Mexico at the Anfra Holiday Motel.

Kenneth and me outside the Anfra Holiday Motel Kenneth and Bobby on the parking lot beside it

While we were sighting seeing the first day we were there, we would park our car, get out, look around and every time, when we would get back to it, it would be dry cleaned! Someone would be there still wiping on it. My husband gave them a tip the first couple of times. After about four or five times he had had enough! He refused to give any of them another tip. One of the young men said something to his cohorts then looked at my husband and called him some dirty names, and walked away! I did not really understand what he actually said but I knew it was not anything nice because of his attitude and the look on his face.

The next day we were told about a man who would drive our car for us and so we could go to the many sites the city had to offer. He became our tour guide.

My husband asked our guide about the young men who dry-cleaned cars before they noticed he was driving for us. He asked him why they did it. He explained that were simply trying to take care of themselves and maybe, their families. He also told us that because we were in a name brand car (a 1965 Cadillac) these young men figured we had money. I also found out that there was no car manufacturing done in the whole country of Mexico, so cars were quite expensive because they were imported. The one we drove cost the big, big bucks in their country.

I had noticed before that they only dry-cleaned certain cars but that had not registered until his explanation. It was also surprising that our car was not being dry-cleaned any more no matter where it was parked. I soon deduced that his presence in our car was the key our being left alone.

We had an opportunity to visit a strong drink making place called Arturo's one day. I am a person who is a teetotaler. Yet, I liked one of theirs! It was called the drink of the house. I told Bobby that I wanted to bring a bottle of it home with us. He would have if I hadn't wanted it to be in a big beautiful jug. The jug held that drink, and *three* others that I couldn't stand!

Bobby wanted to know, "Why do you want all four when you don't like but one?"

"They are so pretty together in that bottle. One is green one is a pretty pinkish red, and two other colors in all in one bottle!" I told him.

"So, I'm to pay $12.00 just to get a **bottle** across the border after we pay for it here?"

"Well, why not?" I asked.

"No well anything. We are not going to buy it! It would be different if you liked one of the others, but you don't even like anything really but that stupid bottle. No."

Or course I didn't ever have a chance to taste the drink again.

What Kenneth remembered most about the trip was, having the chance to play in one pool or another on both sides of the border.

Kenneth, me, Bobby and James Lee
The family; together right after finding out I was pregnant

Bobby Junior is Born

In 1969 I was making all kind of plans to see if I could go to Europe. I am an avid reader. I had read so much about places there and wanted to see some of them. I went to the doctor. When I came away I had reasons to change all my plans. I was expecting another child! I was tickled about the knowledge. I told everyone who would listen. It was in the month of June and at the time our other son James, was visiting with us. James' mother and grandmother had allowed him to stay with us a few days. He and Kenneth were there with Bobby when I returned home from the doctor's office.

At the time Kenneth was nine years old and wanted to be quite helpful. He decided that he had to help me get through the time of my pregnancy. The doctor gave me a book about taking care of myself. Kenneth decided to read it.

After a while I would hear him tell me, "Mom, you are to eat food that will be good for the baby."

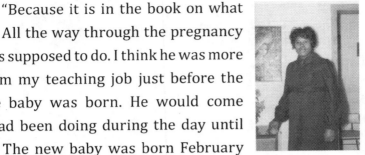

"How do you know what I am supposed to eat?"

"Because it is in the book on what they say you are supposed to do."

All the way through the pregnancy he made it his business to tell me what I was supposed to do. I think he was more relieved than his daddy when I resigned from my teaching job just before the Christmas break in December 1969 before the baby was born. He would come home from school and want to know what I had been doing during the day until the baby came.

The new baby was born February 24, 1970 a few weeks *after* the time the doctor told me he was to be born. I believe I carried him for ten months instead of nine because of when the doctor told me I was pregnant and when he was delivered! He was a hefty fellow at nine pounds eight ounces.

Bobby, Jr.

This beautiful new baby proved to be a real challenge. He was about five months old before he slept from about ten o'clock that night, until about six in the morning! He didn't do it again until he was several months older. I finally put him on a schedule for feeding so I could have some 'down time.' Even then he liked staying up late.

The house we had built down the street from the first home we had built in '61.

We decided to build another home when Bobby Jr. was a few months pass a year old. By the time he was almost two we had already moved into the other house down the street from the first one we had had built. I was very pleased to try out my decorating skills in making it into "our" home.

Kenneth was as helpful as he could be with his brother. But, their being ten years apart sometimes caused problems, mostly for Kenneth. Somehow I believe since the baby was named Bobby Jean Durham, *Junior* he had an edge over his brother. The difference in their ages and, I strongly believe his name gave Bobby Junior, the edge. He would so often blame Kenneth for whatever misconduct they got into.

Bobby Junior's favorite comment when his Daddy would ask them, "Boys, why are you making all that noise?"

"That's Kenneth, Daddy. He is messing with me!"

Their father would always seem to take Bobby Junior's word, no matter how much Kenneth denied it. Many times, it was the very other way around.

I learned that Kenneth was not always the blame by catching Bobby Jr. in the act. I was looking in the door when Bobby Jr. hit his brother because of some-thing. Their father heard Bobby Junior because he started yelling when Ken started toward him, their daddy wanted to know what was going on. Bobby Jr.'s quick answer was, "Kenneth is messing with me, Daddy!"

For a while Kenneth took the blame without much complaint, until he got really fed up.

That was when they would really get into some big spats. Which of course would always be Kenneth's fault if, you listened to Bobby Junior. It didn't get go on too long because by this time was Kenneth started his many extra-circular activities at school and he was not there so much to take the all fall out.

From the time that Bobby Junior first grade he had one babysitter. She crazy about her 'Little Bobby' and, he was aggravated with me or anyone else go stay with "Dor's." He would then get across the street to the house where what he told her but he was usually  **Doris Hand** was a baby until he was enrolled in the was our neighbor Doris Hand. She was so was about her. He would tell me when he in the house that he was going leave us and some toys, put them in his wagon and go Doris lived with her father. (I don't know back by the next mealtime!)

She never seemed too busy to put up with him when he went over. We would just watch him and see what he would do. She and her father would let him play around their house until he, decided he was ready to go back home. She might call me to let me know he was on the way back to the house when he left their place. We would just call each other, laugh and say, "He is on the way there."

Kenneth and Bobby

Kenneth being a teenager by the time Bobby Junior got old enough to go to school he was away at one kind of school activity or the other. He was a football player, basketball player and many other sports except, baseball. He only played baseball in elementary school. He got two of his teeth knocked out at that time. His two teeth at the bottom front were knocked completely down into his mouth!

We were able to secure a marvelous dentist who saved those teeth. Even after they were broken and, tearing some of his gums in the process! The dentist put the teeth back into place and repaired his gums. They healed and I don't think he ever had any trouble with them anymore. From that time on, Kenneth played no more baseball.

His school activities did not bother me at all. I just thought they were some constructive ways to keep him active and his mind busy. What did shake me up was the first time I was made aware that he was thinking about to start dating!

I was in the kitchen cooking dinner one afternoon when he was telling his dad, his aunt who was doing her student teaching in one or the high school's here in town, about a dance he was hoping to go to. He told them what kind of dance it was, or what the name of it was. He then said he had met a girl that he wanted to ask as his date!

Listening in the kitchen I nearly dropped the pan I was holding! Ken was talking about a date, with a girl? Did he *really* say he was going to take a, date? I even lost my breath for a minute. My son was talking about dating a girl. Boy, I was stunned. I came slowly to myself and just tried to keep listening to them talking about the activity.

The dance happened, and it didn't kill me, nor did the world come to an end. We weren't inundated with girlfriends either. He seemed so much less of a player than some of his close buddies that I knew about.

He even acted as the 'go to' fellow when a couple of his friends were having trouble with their girlfriends. I was flabbergasted, especially, when a couple of friends came to the house one day **before** school to get advice on what to do with one of his relationship! I personally wondered if the kid had lost him mind.

Kenneth really did well in school. His grades were acceptable all the way through. If they had not been he would not have had the opportunity to always participate in the sports. We never had to get on him about bringing up his grades. At graduation he had offers to take scholarships from several very good colleges to play football. After visiting several of the places with him as we all checked them out, and being treated so nicely, he decided to go to Texas Christian University in Fort Worth, Texas.

He left in June right after school was out. He went, because he got a job there in Fort Worth where he was to work all summer before school started in the fall. Before this time I had heard of mothers crying when their first child left home. I had never thought anything about it. But, I learned firsthand about the phenomenon and how they felt!

He had his own little black car, a Cougar, to drive by then. We packed up his car and ours to take all his stuff to his place there. We took the drive up following him. When we got there we put his stuff in the apartment where he was going to stay. After that we went to visit other family members in the Dallas area, he followed us over there in his car.

After visiting with family, we left him at his aunt's home. Then we left to come back home. I was still ok during all this time. It was when we made it back to Beaumont, Texas just about 17miles away from home that I burst!

I kept thinking, "Lord, I left my baby in Fort Worth. He is gone for good! He probably won't ever stay with us again except just to visit! "BOO-hoo!" I burst into tears feeling really low, at that point. I cried for a while. I got over it after, even though the abandoned feeling lasted for a time.

The house behind Angie, Chan and Clarence

Repairs to Our Home Place

By this time Mama had added two small bedrooms rooms and a bathroom to the house by this time. It was after Big Mama moved to Grand Prairie to live with Aunt Sis her other daughter. Mama used Big Mama old house to add these much needed additions. This increased the size of the house to four bedrooms, with *a bathroom*! Mama got a decent sized house after all the years of needing one. (It seemed ironic that most of the children were now gone except for the young ones.)

In the early 70's it was obvious that the home place was badly in need of some repairs. All of us gathered at Laura's house in Dallas for a meeting. We outlined the things that we thought needed doing on the house and how we were going to pay for it. There was some money that we had received from an oil company for the lease of the land. One of the men in the area rented the land out front of the homestead for farming. A few geological shots of some kind had been also made on the property that we had gotten a bit of money for. All this added up to a little under $2000. We were planning to use that to begin the work.

We decided who would do what, and, what Mama could handle by herself. She had said she would see about getting someone to repair the flooring in the kitchen as soon as possible since they were in such bad shape. When we discussed what was to be done and the cost. We also figured it would be more than we had.

It was then suggested by Elouise that each of us needed to contribute about $200 apiece to the kitty we had set up. I was the person selected to find a place to deposit the kitty and keep the records of what happened. Everything went along well until most of the work done. I drew a crude drawing of what had been done and a sketch of what still was proposed.

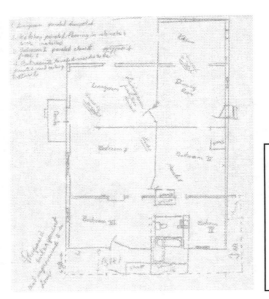

This crude drawing of Mama's floor plans that pointed out what we had gotten done by July 29, 1930 with the money we had gathered by then.

This drawing was sent to all the members of the family with thanks and to show the proposed renovations that we still wanted get done.

Though we were going forward with the repairs on the house when we had gotten to the point of adding to the part of the house where they had connected Big Mama's to the rest of it when we hit a couple of snags. The first one was that we were not being paid by the companies that were getting gravel from our land!

It, the gravel they were getting, was going out from our property from another part of the land away from the house in between the property of my sister's land and another of our neighbors in the community. Mama didn't know, nor did any of us, that they were still hauling it. They paid someone else the money that was due us!

When they were made aware of the error, they dug a road leading to the dig site that actually went by our house to get the gravel. Afterward, they stated that the cost of building the new entryway took up the remainder of the fees they had allotted as payment for the gravel. We got no money from them and we could not go any further because by then our house repair "kitty" was depleted!

There were things that still needed to be done but we lacked the 'where-with-all' to get them done. So, we just had the table the work. Though the house lacked a lot it was by far much better than it had been. The kitchen had a sink with a cabinet beneath it. There was a new stove and a few more cabinets in the area on the front, and back walls for storage in the kitchen area plus the dining area.

What did surprise us was that the old messed up sink with cabinets that we had replaced and put outside. When we came back the next time **Mama**, had somehow managed to get it back into the house! She placed it on the wall across from the refrigerator in the dining area. It was in the way a bit since it protruded into the doorway. We left it there because if Mama wanted it back in the house that much, we were not going to move it again. We wondered how she managed to put it back alone. We didn't know, and didn't ask how she got back there. We didn't try to remove it again; we got her message without her saying a word.

Cotis Is Taken from Us in 1975!

Mama and all the family had a real trauma during the summer of 1975. Brothers, Cotis, Carlton, Willie C and a number of their friends went on one of their many fishing trips. It was an activity that all three of my brothers enjoyed and most of the times to stayed the whole day. This one was especially interesting because it was some kind of fishing tournament.

Going out on the water Cotis and Carlton were on the same fishing boat. Willie C was on the boat with two other friends. While they were there Carton reported later, that Cotis who was steering the boat with the stick and all of a sudden he stood up, and the boat went into a tail spin. They all fell into the water. Carlton and the other man were picked up not too long after they had fallen. My brother, Cotis was not found! They searched that day and for almost the whole next week before finding his body!

My brother, Cotis

No one could ever imagine, without having gone through an experience similar to this, what it is like for those closest to the person, whose person/body is lost! The fact that you are in limbo about your loved one is most excruciating! You want to hope he'll be found alive, but realizing that the expectation is that he is already dead, make you feel like you are on pins and needles. The totally uncertainty is heart wrenching!

Willie C and Carlton, who were with him at the time when he fell out of the boat, suggested that he may have had a heart attack when he stood up. He stood at the stick a minute then he just tumbled over the back of the boat as the others went over the sides. They looked and looked for him all the rest of that day to no avail

During the time we were waiting to find out what had happened to him, I was working at my job teaching school children and trying to hold it together while working with them. I lost it only once during that time.

I was in the teacher's lounge and the Supervisor made a simple comment and lost it. I was talking to someone and she walked in. She was there for a minute when she looked my way frowned and said, "Honey you look like you just lost your best buddy. Liven' it up some, girl!"

I just burst into tears and ran from the room. Several of the other teachers who knew about the fact that my brother was still missing explained to her why I was a bit down. I thought I had been holding up pretty good. But after her comments, I had to be alone for a time before going back into the classroom.

It was another day or so after that, before we heard that they had found my brother's body. They found that he had been dead since he'd fallen out of the boat or very soon after. It took almost a whole week to find him.

For the funeral the family gathered at Cotis' and Jane's, home. Mama was present as well. As she had always done, she showed a calm demeanor with a prayer on her lips when she came to Providence Baptist Church in Dallas for the service. Being a mother myself I know it was really hard to lose a child. I know her faith in God is what helped her make it through.

The funeral was also a release. It was his funeral that helped me to realize that funerals are **for the families and loved ones**. It helps them find a bit of closure. It may be a memorial for the one gone on, but the family needs it. I know that after so many days the harrowing experience of not knowing, we really did get a start on recovery after the funeral.

Carlton was a bit of a wild one on a normal basis, but when he watched Cotis go down something happened to him. Cotis' death really accelerated some of his bad decisions. Even at the funeral itself. I come to realize that he was quite affected by his passing the way he did.

Mama was sad but standing on God's Word, as she had at so many other times. The singing that she always did while she was moving around the house she was still doing, only now it was voicing her sadness, and her need of God's counseling and comfort. I feel we all did.

Her favorite saying, "The Lord will provide" for her and the family, in this instance as He had always done for her so many others, proved true. We came through our troubled times.

My Texas Brogue, Takes a Hike!

The fall of 1981 brought another real challenge into **my life**, and the lives of some of the members of the family!

I went to a gathering in October of 1981, at one of our neighbor's home. Bobby's fraternity brother was hosting a gathering for the brothers and their 'significant others'. There was smoking going on. I think I may have smoked some myself. I found out later I was allergic to cigarette smoke! Even then, I had no idea what the results of my trying to smoke, and being in a room where lots of others did too would have on me. When I awoke the next morning, October 18, 1981, I had a sore throat and was a bit hoarse as well.

That day, a Sunday, happened to be a busy one for me. I had to teach a Sunday school class, sing lead for the choir during our regular morning church services that morning and that evening at 3:00 P.M. the church was celebrating its anniversary. I was the Emcee for the event as well as the soloist for the choir. I barely made it through the day, even with all the home remedies I could think of to shore me up!

By Monday My throat was so very scratchy and my voice quite deep. Yet, I knew I needed to to keep up my attendance at school, so I went on to school anyway. By the end of the day I was speaking with great difficulty and, in a scratchy whisper. In spite of the problems I continued for two more days trying to teach, hoping it would go away. It didn't. In fact, it just got much worse.

Then, I decided to see my regular family doctor. After examining me he prescribed medication for me and told me, "Take the medicine, it will help but, you need to rest your voice for a while."

I took the medicine but, I felt I needed to continue working because I had used up too many of my sick days. I had been sick so much the years before. I wanted to increase the number of my unused sick days for the year for a time when I figured I would really need them. My throat wasn't so sore by then and, I was feeling all right everywhere else. I kept working for the rest of the week though my voice was really sounding much worse as the days went by. By the end of the week, my voice was only a very rough whisper. I was writing most of my instructions for the class on the chalkboard and making sign for others. My voice did not get better. The students were so much nicer since they knew I was having trouble talking.

By October 25, my voice could best be described as sounding like a poor grade, scratchy record that also had a few chips or holes in it! It was also obvious to the listener that talking was a very laborious and sometimes painful task for me. Many would try and help me out by supplying the word/words they thought I was trying to say. My students did so as well they were awfully nice during this time, too. Even so by the end of the day I was bleary-eyed with exhaustion. I was also quite worried about what was happening to me. I had had laryngitis before but it had never lasted so long or caused me so much pain. I saw my doctor again.

He suggested that I see an ear, nose and throat specialist here in town. I made an appointment to see him, but it took another week before he could actually see me. During the examination he asked me to say the traditional "aaaaah." I tried but it was more of a hissing-non-sound.

His comment was, "You've really got it bad!"

He then asked me what my family doctor had done. I told him as best I could what my doctor had done and how long it had been going on. He then told me he too, was confused about why the problem continued. I felt that he thought I should have been over the laryngitis by this time. From his obviously puzzled reaction I left his office even more concerned than I had been up to this point even though he gave me another prescription, he made the comment, "**Maybe** this medication will help clear up your problem."

When I got home I called my family doctor's office again, because had I decided to see him to tell him what was still going on with my voice. I decided to go that day as a walk-in, and when I got there I had to talk to one of his co-workers.

The doctor I talked to commented after listening to me and finding out how long it had been going on, listed a couple of possible problems or ailment the symptoms I had might indicate. Hearing those suggestions didn't bring any feeling of relief or comfort. In fact, I was quite shaken. The suggestions were quite serious and a bit strange to me. By this time I had already decided it was time for me to take time off to "rest my voice."

I was really worried, not only because of what he had told me but also, when I would be talking, the phrases I used would not necessarily be the ones I had been accustomed to using before. Then, there were the times I would be speaking and some of the words or parts of the words I intended to say didn't become vocal. The sounds just would not come out! I really sounded like an old record/disc with a hole in it! Friends and people I talked to were constantly saying things **for,** me because they could tell that by now, it hurt to talk.

Someone I hadn't seen in a while heard me and suggested I go to a place called the Diagnostic Clinic in the Medical Center of Houston, Texas. Normally, Reading, sewing, and watching television had always been things I enjoyed when I got the chance to do them before, but not this time, in the state I was in. I was having a trying time just living with myself.

After talking to my doctor about it he helped me get an appointment there since the symptoms suggested some weird named disease. I was given the date of November 11, 1981 to check in. By now I was thinking all kinds of weird things especially, since by this time I was being told funny things about my speech patterns. Even my doctor who had known me since 1960 told me I sounded like a foreigner when I went to pick up my medical records. The beautician I had been going to for years also told me the same thing about my voice when I got my hair done.

On the eleventh, when I checked into the Diagnostic Center, my efforts to speak were much less painful than they had been for days. My speech was easier for others to understand, but the admitting physician while examining me, turned to my husband, and asked him, "How long has your wife been speaking English?"

I was shocked because I had not taken note of the difference in the sound of my voice up to this point. I frankly was just getting used to the fact that it wasn't hurting as much as it had been when I tried to talk. On top of that all the words came out.

I answered the doctor myself. "But, Doctor, I only know English! I have never spoken anything else! Well, except in a couple classes of in French taken in college that I can't recall too well."

"You mean you only speak English?" The doctor asked. Then turned to my husband and asked him. "You mean she is an American?"

My husband told him, "Yes she is, we both came from the same place in Texas."

"You really are a Texan?"

"Yes Sir, I am a native Texan."

"Then where did the accent come from?"

"That is the reason for our being here, along with the other problems she was having with her voice and throat." My husband told the doctor.

The doctor then asked me to try and explain

"Well, until a day or so ago it hurt more than you can ever imagine, just getting out a complete sentence. Now, it only hurts a little. I would have had instances of speaking and not all of the words were vocalized. I've also been told the symptoms I have been having could indicate some very serious muscle deteriorating diseases."

"Frankly lady, I've never heard of something like this! Your voice is too strong today for some of the things you are talking about. You may be hoarse, but you have a very noticeable accent!'

"I am going to have a few tests done in the next few days, and I'll want you to see a few other doctors here. The first one I want you to see is our neurosurgeon."

That was just the *beginning* of a series of encounters with at least 13 doctors! The admitting doctor would come into my room; introduce a person and say, "Talk to him or her."

I like people. So, I very seldom ever found it difficult to find something to say, especially since by now it was not difficult to do, I had become quite a talker in my adult years. The only thing that was amazing to me, as well as it was for the doctor, was that I had a distinct accent, one that even I could hear and thought odd!

The doctor would then ask the newcomer, "Where do you think she is from?"

The answers were as numerous as the doctors. Their answers were that I was from Eastern Europe, the Caribbean, Jamaica and other places. Then the doctor would then say, "She is a native Texan!"

After that I'd have to go over the history of the things that led up to the condition that had brought me to the center. Most would then sit and talk with me for a time. I think many just did so out of curiosity and some trying to speculate about my condition. I don't know what they expected.

The neurosurgeon got to be a regular visitor throughout the days I was there. He'd just come in, sit down and begin talking or asking questions. He would stay from ten to thirty minutes at a time. I assumed later that he was making observations. During the other times he was not there, I was undergoing lots of tests of one kind or another. Some they told me what they were with letters and others they did I never knew what they were. Some of them were EEG, MRI, brain scan, and various physical exams by, throat specialist, a speech therapist, a diagnostician, another neurologist and at least seven other doctors.

Their conclusion: "Lady we've never heard of anything like it!"

I continued to feel much better but the strange accent was still there, only it was changing slightly. It sounded quite Middle Eastern, even to me for while, then it shifted to a more Caribbean tone.

During my stay at Diagnostic Medical Center, family members and friends came to visit and I was their reactions to the new sound of my voice. My brother-in-law James Artis, who had also been my classmate in high school came to see me and brought his wife, Delores, one day while Bobby and Bobby, Jr. were gone.

He spoke. Asked how I was. When I answered, he got this strange look on his face. He stayed at the door. Delores sat on the bed next to me and we talked about how things were for me and a lot of other things. I was so happy to be able to talk without any pain I didn't notice for awhile that James said absolutely nothing else to me after I started talking. The hoarseness was almost gone but the accent was there **in spades!** I finally noticed and told him to come on in, but he mumbled something and stayed near the door.

Delores called me back, later that evening after they had gone home. "Eddie I know you felt it, James was really affected by your voice. He was scared!"

"He was scared? I felt something was bothering him, but scared? It never occurred to me."

"Yes, of you, or rather your new voice, he called Sis as soon as he got home told her that you were really sick or something. You sounded like another person altogether! He said he didn't know what to think. Your laugh was the only thing that was the same"

"Were you scared?" I asked her.

"Me? No, you do sound different and everything, but I think it's kind of cute. I'll have to get used to you sounding like that, though."

James' reaction was just the first of the many different reactions people gave me after hearing my voice.

I called my own mother after talking with Delores and talked to her. She took the difference in my accent with only the comment, "Honey, if you can now speak more easily and with no pain, it may be the Lord's will for you. But, I must say you do sound different."

My stepfather teased me, "Well, I guess you wore out your old voice and the Lord had to provide you with somebody else's accent to replace it!"

After I finished laughing, Uncle Luke then told me, "I told you, you talked too much!"

Meanwhile...

The doctor who checked me into the Center and the neurosurgeon I saw so much of, told me they saw nothing they could diagnose. Since I was feeling quite well I was able to be released. The release however, came only, after I had been given all the tests and exams they could think of, as well as, see all the doctors they could think of to send me to. They, the admitting doctor and the neurosurgeon, asked I could make a follow-up visit to the Center in February, of 1982.

I went back to school. Boy, there were many different reactions to my change of accent! My students, co-workers, the parents of my students, friends and people I met for the first time, they all want to know what happened to me.

When I did go back to the Medical Center in February, I was told in essence, by both doctors that they were mainly curious to see whether the accent that I had acquired when I was admitted to the Center earlier would still be in place. It was. It was only clearer and smoother, but still in place!

They wanted me to check into a neurological hospital there in Houston so that they could investigate the phenomenon some more. My husband had decided that he liked the accent and didn't care how I got it, especially since I no longer had any difficulty talking.

It was his opinion that I didn't need to worry about it anymore.

Besides he told me later, "We would probably end up paying for their curiosity and study, while still not finding the answer as to why. Besides you can't afford to be absent from your job any longer without losing pay." That settled the matter.

A couple of weeks after I was released from the Center in November, I went home to Mama's to visit, because Uncle Luke was in the hospital at Palestine, Texas.

Mama's reaction to my accent in person, was just as she took everything, with quiet meekness. She was very uplifted that I was feeling so much better.

Her only comment was, "The Lord works in mysterious ways."

Uncle Luke Passes, Mama Is Widowed Again

While I was visiting Uncle Luke, a nurse who had heard me talking to Mama and Uncle Luke, asked the usual questions I got almost everywhere I went in those days.

She wanted to know where I was born and reared and the like. After hearing the story she told us the next day she had asked her pastor to pray for me because she thought I may have been possessed!

I thanked her, and told her, "Continue praying, though I do not feel I have been possessed. I need all the prayers I can get!"

Mama and Uncle Luke just smiled. They told me not to be upset by her remarks.

After Uncle Luke got out of the out of the hospital he and Mama went to Dallas for a few days. While they were there, he decided to go to church with Georgia. That in itself was unusual for Uncle Luke. He never went to church except for funerals, but not only did he go when they got there, Uncle Luke, decided to join the church!

Georgia said that he told her that he felt the Lord was in her life, and he wanted to join the church where she was going even though he wanted his membership sent to the church Mama attended at home. The church where he joined was, the True Way Church of God in Christ on that Thursday evening. He told the pastor know that though he was joining there, he wanted his membership to be at Mama's Church at home, The Owens Chapel Church of God in Christ.

His actions were a totally real surprise to the family, especially since in all the years they had been married he would just sit and watch Mama and her children go to church. He would also make comments about her and our attendance that were not always complimentary. It was the answer to so many of Mama's prayers. She had always hoped that he would accept God in his life. It was another instance where we saw that God answers prayers

Mama was also right in the comment she made that said "The Lord moves in mysterious ways," because Uncle Luke's illness was still with him. He would not survive the illness! It was not too long after this their trip to Dallas that that Uncle Luke passed away.

Uncle Luke's passing on the 28th of March 1982, left Mama completely alone at home because by this time all the children were all were old enough to be gone. Mama, I don't think, had **ever** been by herself. She had been with someone all her life. From the time of her teen years she had had a husband, older people and children around her. Now the youngest, Luke Junior, had graduated more than ten years before in 1971. Her baby girl, Lean, had graduated a few years earlier. They were the last of the children who had been left at home. So Uncle Luke's death really left her in a very uncommon situation.

Venus Lean   **Luke Junior**

The two youngest of our crew

Even though on the outside Mama was her regular self, Uncle Luke's death left her very unsettled. As far as her health and her mental well being were concerned. Being home alone, for her, wasn't good. She stayed there that way for only little a while. I can't remember exactly how long it was. I would go see her and my in-laws fairly often, but my siblings in Dallas could go a bit more often. My sister, Laura, "Earth mother" for the family, was kept aware of the fact that she was having health problems by the closest neighbor to Mama's house.

Mama's Moves to Dallas

After Uncle Luke died, Mama stayed at home for a while alone. We, my family, visited but she seemed to be her usual self when we were there. She even bought some more furniture for the house. It was the purchase of that furniture that brought another real memorable experience with my acquired accent.

It was the incident that happened at in Palestine, Texas and it still remains very vivid in memory, for me. Mama had bought some furniture at a store there. She had paid for it, the full quoted price. I knew that because, I had given her the money for the **last** payment. Yet, she was still receiving bills even after it had been paid. I was really pissed. I went home, took Mama to the store to see if we could get it straightened out.

I went into the store with Mama and was trying to explain to the clerk at the store what was going on. I asked questions about this, trying to find out why, since I knew Mama had already paid for the furniture, she was still getting bill. The clerk just sat and stared at me strangely. She didn't seem to have heard, or understood, a word I had said. She then interrupted me mid-sentence to inquire of me, "Excuse me Lady but where are you from?"

I quickly replied "I live in Port Arthur, Texas, what…."

She stopped even pretending to be listening to my complaint and started questioning me about my accent.

"But Lady, you don't sound like someone from Texas."

"But I am a Texan and I was born right across Trinity River in a community near Fairfield. But, we are not talking about my accent, I want to know what has happened to your records? I know Mama has paid for that furniture!"

"I'm sorry Ma'am, but you sound so different!"

Then my husband, Bobby came up. "Excuse me Ma'am, I am with these ladies. Would you please get the manager?"

After a talk with the manager himself, my husband finally got them to discuss the matter that had brought us into the store!

Even then neither of them seemed to want to hear anything except my explaining about how my voice changed, and when!

It was only after my husband and Mama, explained reason we were there that the matter was finally settled. Even then they still had their questions. When they were answered they were still skeptical.

While my family was doing well, with me just suffering the 'Separation Syndrome' because Kenneth had gone away college in Fort Worth. Mama had not been faring so well. I felt so bad that we didn't know.

Laura, was the one Mama's neighbor, and our childhood friend, called when her problems got worse. Mama was having problems with muscle spasms and couldn't take care of herself. She was also having other physical ailments as well.

Laura got a friend of hers there in Dallas to go down by ambulance and pick Mama up and bring her to Dallas where she could be cared for. This was after she had some really bad bouts with her health.

Even after she got better, she decided to stay with Laura and her family. They convinced her mostly because those in Dallas found it easier having her there with them and, she liked being there too. One of them would go down home to get things she wanted or needed from the house as she continued to stay with Laura. After a while the house with no one there and she had gotten all she needed folks in the area took from it too.

When Mama got to be a permanent resident, is when Laura's mother-hen tendencies and the feeling of herself as the one who was in charge, really showed up with us. In the fact, the times when she always seemed to be *happiest* was when Mama, her own children, as well as all of us, her brothers and sisters, our spouses and children were gathered at her home with other families and friends she had invited were there, too.

My Accent Causes Problems, Again

Though Mama was going through her difficulties I was having some of my own.

I have never thought of myself as being possessed but I have had some memorable experiences because of the accent change.

One of the times was the time I was visiting Oneida, one of my sisters-in-law's home, while one of her husband's sisters and someone else was there, too. One of her husband's sisters had attended college with me. She and I did quite a bit of talking. While she and I were talking Oneida, seemed to be a bit uncomfortable and, she did not say very much, to me, which was so unlike her.

I mentioned it after her other visitors were gone.

Her response was a bit defensive, "I told Laura you had had a voice transplant! How is anyone supposed to explain the difference in the way your voice is now and what it was?"

I had no comeback for her.

My husband and our younger son in jest would allow people we met for the first time to believe I was from someplace else, just, to see what they would say. They said they really got such a kick out of it because many of the people really believed them.

The first time they did it, we were in a department store and I was looking for a blouse. After being dissatisfied with what I had seen, the clerk offered to get some others from the storeroom. Those were no more pleasing to me.

My husband quipped, "Bobby, you'd think she'd be so glad to be in a free country like ours, that she'd be able to like some of the nice things we have here, don't you think?"

"You know, Dad, I was thinking the same thing. She's seen all kinds of stuff and hasn't liked any of it. That's an awful shame!" Bobby Junior replied winking at his father.

The clerk asked my husband, "How long has she been in this country?"

He and Bobby, Junior looked at each other and grinned widely, "She's been here long enough."

"Thank you, Ma'am. I guess we'll go, since she doesn't like anything here. "

When we got outside, the two of them could contain themselves no longer. After they stopped laughing long enough to speak, Bobby Junior said, "She really thought Mom was a foreigner!"

That was the first time but, it was by no means the last. They pulled some kind of stunt like that. There were other incidents but this one stayed in my memory because it was so first.

There have also been times I've been stopped while talking to friends in grocery stores, elevators, and many other places where I was heard speaking. People have been curious about my 'original' home.

When I say I am a native Texan who acquired this accent after a bout with laryngitis. They usually don't believe me and, actually some have accused me of being a liar. It is at those times that even I feel like just going along with them, about where my birthplace was. But I never did, I knew I could actually pretend to be from somewhere else. But, I would be lying so, I never have. One other reason was that I would not be able to describe 'the place' I supposedly came from in anymore detail more than someone who Just visit the place since they would be in another country. I have only had limited trips outside the dear state of Texas!

There was one time when the accent I had acquired in '81 really caused a serious problem for me. This problem had with it the possibility of my being deported!

My son, Kenneth, was discomforted, too because he was with me. It happened when the company he worked for transferred him from the place he worked to Boca Raton, Florida to be assistant manager of a store there.

It was in the month of August, and I decided to go with them when they went to look for housing in the area. While we were there they decided to take a pleasure Day cruise to the Bahamas and I went along.

Getting aboard to go there was quite simple. All I needed to go, was a driver's license and a voter registration card. During the trip over we had lots of fun me being able to read or talk with the people on board. Kenneth decided he wanted to try the slot machines. They had them on the ship, though you couldn't play them until some miles out into the Gulf. He tried a few times, lost all the quarters he had. He then asked me if I wanted to try them. I refused I told him what I tell everybody about taking a chance with my money. "Honey when I put my money on something, I know what I am going to get. It is not a **chance** on something."

I did let him have a quarter or two I had in my purse. He even won a few dollars!

While there on the island, The Grand Bahamas, I did have a few people that asked if I were from one of the other islands. But, I only thought of it as nothing more than a way to get acquainted. I thought nothing of it. While there I just had a lovely and enjoyable stay.

Now when I returned to Miami, Florida it was another story all together!

We docked back in Miami around 4:00 P. M. that evening, the immigration lady there who looked my identification material had heard me talking to my son and his wife, while we were waiting our turn to be checked out.

She asked, "Are you an alien, ma'am?'

I answered smiling. I was thinking about the movie *"**Alien**"* that had been shown while we were coming over. And, it was a movie that my younger son had been talking about before I left home.

"No ma'am."

"I noticed that you have an accent. Where were you born?" She asked.

I answered, "Ma'am I had a long bout with laryngitis that left me with this accent. I was born in a small town in Central Texas."

"Lady, people don't just acquire accents. Sit over there!"

Kenneth and his wife were told they could go.

At first I was just curious about what she wanted, but I was left sitting for ages so long I became quite agitated.

Then, she began questioning me over and over again! Many of the questions were ones she asked over and over. I had in my possession what I was told that I needed for the passage into and out of, the islands of the Bahamas in fact I had been there to another one of the islands before with my husband and Bobby Junior. We had gone to Mexico, and I had even been to Canada using the same items for identification before. Even though I had the same information with me, and showed it, and many other things that I had in my bag that indicated where I lived. I had to answer these questions, the same ones over and over again.

After I had done that politely for hours, I became aggravated.

"Ma'am do you want to call the superintendent of schools in Port Arthur, the principal of Sam Houston Elementary School where I work and have worked since 1960, or an officer of the police department, anyone you choose. They can tell you I am a native born Texan!"

"Lady, there are hundreds of people trying to sneak into this country every day!" She retorted angrily.

She turned and walked briskly away leaving me standing in the large empty room.

I went in the same direction she went to leave. The ship we were in on had docked at between 4:00-4:30 P. M. and I had been detained until about 9:00 P.M. that night!

Bobby, Senior's and Bobby, Junior's summary of the encounter when they were told was rather cryptic.

"We always said you talked a lot. Well......" Bobby Junior remarked.

His daddy finished for him' "If you had kept your mouth shut when you were on that ship, you would not have been in so much trouble!" as they both burst into laughter.

That story has been repeated so many times since then.

I was so shook up after this experience I obtained a passport as soon as I could after returning home to Port Arthur. I hoped that when and if, I traveled outside the country again I would have no trouble at all.

The fact that I had my passport just encouraged me to explore whenever the opportunity presented itself.

Picture taken for passport

Bobby Junior's and My Trip to Florida

These pictures were taken at a Rest Stop and of Bobby Junior making an emergency call, at a roadside box on the Florida highway. We had both been curious about them since we had seen them on our first trip there. On this trip a family on the road needed help, and he was glad to oblige.

We, Bobby Senior, Bobby Junior and I, had planned a family visit to Kenneth's in Florida again. Especially, since we had liked the places we had seen on our previous visits. Bobby Senior found that he would not be able to go with us.

Bobby Junior and I had the opportunity to take the trip by car from Port Arthur to Florida by ourselves! It happened because the principals of the Port Arthur School District had had their schedules changed. They would no longer be off all summer as they had been during the years before. They would have only a couple of weeks off with the new schedules the Director of Schools gave them. They would be making books of guidelines for teachers and students or some such busy work they assigned.

Bobby Junior and I decided we could go to see Kenneth and his wife anyway, as well as travel around Florida on our own. Bobby Senior gave us his blessings to 'go-it alone,' especially since I had traveled to San Antonio and back, as well as to Dallas and back all on my own not too long before then. He just instructed us to be careful, as well as giving us all kinds of other instructions, on taking care.

Bobby Junior was to be back-up driver but I did almost all of it because, he had just hurt his shoulder in a sporting activity and it was still quite sore. He was just like his brother Kenneth, had been before him, into all kinds of sports. The only one he didn't try that Kenneth did was basketball. His injury was from his power lifting. He did provide some help along the way in spite of the soreness.

While we were there we had a chance to travel over much of the whole state of Florida. We saw new fruit trees and large ones. We also had good times at the travel stations along the interstate highways and toll roads. We also got visit other sights and shopping malls along the way that were fascinating places to stop and visit.

We took the opportunity to visit quite a few. We didn't have money to buy all the stuff we wanted. But, we got to see them that, in itself was lots of fun for me. It was not so bad for Bobby Junior either.

A palm root hut and a Yacht club with lots of fancy boats
All seen on the drive in the Keys

Visiting with Ken and his wife was most enjoyable especially since we got to make tours all around the state. One day we even decided to see if we could get to the Key West, at the end of the Keys in one day. Even the beginning of the trip was an experience. The most fascinating part of it for me was going through Miami and passing the toll booths, doing like one of my favorite TV characters, tossing my money into the bin like he did on the show.

On the way down we stopped at every interesting stop we could. We were not able to make it all the way to Key West on that trip because it would have caused a few problems. However, we did experience a very eventful day. We turned around at Key Largo.

On that day Bobby Junior was wearing his outfit that made him look like someone on "The Beverly Hillbillies" even down to the cowboy boots.

These are two of the scenes taken along the Keyes with Bobby in front of one of them.

On the adventure we did get to see our first shark, see Miami as it is seem on some television shows and visit a beach where there were nude bathers! We had certainly never seen that before!

We saw a car place that Bobby Junior was enthralled with. It had lot of nice looking cars and some **weird** looking ones. He loved it and I was not completely bored. We loved our time with Kenneth but our tours around the state of Florida were for us, totally amazing. Our coming didn't stop their having to be at work so during the day we just explored. It was a fun and awesome time for both us.

On the way back to Texas we had a few more firsts. I got to drive across Lake Pontchartrain on the Toll Causeway was to New Orleans, Louisiana, when we had gone there before Bobby Senior was driving. Bobby Junior and I made a brief visit to the Superdome. We took the tour of it because it was tops on the list to really see since we had never seen it before. It really appealed to us. The time we had visited New Orleans before with Bobby Senior, the Superdome had not been built.

This was what we saw going across Lake Pontchartrain into New Orleans. It was a delightful experience.

Once we reached the area where the dome was, we had to drive around to find a parking place. We finally found one, got out and went in. It was not a day that anything special was going on in Dome except for other visiting tourist like us who wanted to see this much publicized place.

Once our tour was over, we took out the camera to show folks that we had actually been there. We also saw a replica of the Dome done much like a cake. We only stayed for a few hours but we enjoyed them. We both remembered the time we had gone to New Orleans. Bobby was much younger and he thought it was quite funny that I didn't think he should have gone on his little visit to one of the most unusual streets there, in this well known city, at night with his Dad. I had stayed in the hotel room and was really thought he should not have gone.

This is the replica that was shown on the inside of the Dome. I was taking pictures as Bobby Junior drove out of New Orleans

We took pictures around the famous Superdome. I took Him and he took me

Our stay in the jazzy city was so exhilarating. The last hours of traveling home from Louisiana was just a time, especially for me, of finding one mall or shopping spot after another that I could explore. In spite of the fact that I didn't have the money for all that shopping, I enjoyed it all.

It was a really good trip!

One that both of us still remember with fondness.

We Travelled with Mama

One that gets to know me well soon learns that traveling is an experience that I usually really enjoy. I also knew that Mama enjoyed it too. The next very memorable travel experience I had was with Mama.

Since Mama was living with Laura it made things easier for most of her children because most of them lived in and around Dallas. Only Evelyn and I were good distance away. Evelyn was still in California, and I was in Port Arthur. Mama really liked being there since being there since she got to travel all over the United States for meetings that her church was involved in.

There were many places Mama got a chance to enjoy going on trips to as she traveled to places that her church went to for conventions. She was able to visit more than one city in California, go to Miami, Florida, Philadelphia, Pennsylvania, Chicago, Illinois, the Bahamas, Arkansas, New Orleans, Louisiana, St Louis, and Branson Missouri to name a few. She also went to Denver, Colorado another time or too with my sisters, and to Memphis, Tennessee any number of times, I even went with then there a few times, too.

Mama and my sisters also came to Port Arthur for programs I planned at our church. We sang together for concerts that were activities for the Women's Missionary Society at the church I belong to. I even planned it so that Mama had to lead a song or two on a couple of occasions! No one ever asked her to sing with any of the groups of her children who sang before. I knew she could and did sing all the time. She had more than one group that some of her children had sung with. She had boys who sang and girls too. She loved it! I even made here a dress just like ours when they were in Port Arthur.

Mama sitting in front of all of her daughters except, Evelyn who was in California, those pictured Are Georgia Mae Ellis, Venus Lean Bridges, Me, Laura Lee Goosby and Elouise Rider

Our baby sister Lean was the pianist for us. Even though Lean and I lead a few songs Georgia Mae, was the real leader for the group. I had had an opportunity to sing along with our brothers in the quartet they had when I was in Dallas for the summer, Georgia and Lean had sung together, and Lean, Georgia and I sang solos often, too. The three of us had done so from our childhood. Elouise and Laura though good singers had only sung with us and in choirs, except for when Elouise lived in Los Angeles for a short time.

There was a time or two when Mama came to Port Arthur to stay with me and my family for a few days. She also would also stay a few days at some of her other children's homes but, we all knew she **only** thought of Laura's house, as home. She was glad to visit for a few days with one, or the other of us, but we knew that in a short while she was going to want to back HOME, and home to her was with Laura, and **not** with either one of us, or at the old home place. She would make sure you were aware of that.

After Mama went to stay at Laura's there were times that Laura decided to take short trips either alone or with James, her husband. We knew how she felt about Laura's leaving her for these trips. She was like a child whose parents had gone off and left her and did not tell her she was gone! For many days she would tell us Laura didn't need to go, and on others occasions she would just seem dissatisfied with the world, for the first few days.

She even caused a bit of a disturbance at one of the times when Laura and James were gone. She was to staying with Evelyn. What she did upset all of us, even me, and I was not even in town at the time. She just walked off without telling Evelyn where she was going! They looked for her for hours in all the places they could think of. She was gone long enough that the police were even called. They then joined in on the search using cars and helicopters.

Georgia's daughter, Recenda (Cindy), was called and finally gave everyone an idea of where to look for her and decided to look there herself. She went to the place she and Mama had been to a number of occasions before. Mama had said she wanted to go back there and Cindy had put her off. It was a place called *Chuck E Cheese*! That is where Cindy found Mama. She brought her home.

Mama never seemed to feel it was any big deal. For us it was a very trying experience! To Mama, it had been fun. She would tell anyone who would listen about it.

After that time when Mama talked to other folk about it, she showed by her demeanor that she had not the least bit of remorse about the turmoil she may have caused. My husband thought she seemed a bit proud of what she had done.

Lean   **Ausie**

We Loose Lean and Ausie

It was not too long after the sisters and Mama made here where we all sang at our church again, that Lean had a stroke. It was the kind of stroke that made her unable to speak or to eat on her own. She had to have a feeding tube placed in her stomach. She to be put in a place we referred to as a nursing home. The medical folks labeled it as something else, but the place was not somewhere we wanted her to be. But since she was unable to care for herself, and the nature of her ailment made it unlikely that any of us could do it properly if we had been able to invite her home with us. None of us had been around a person with a feeding tube more than for a visit let alone knew how to care for a person on one. This for us was a new and traumatic occurrence. So she had to stay there.

She was placed there before the laws about what grade of cleanliness was given, or strengthened in this state. The place where she was assigned was not nearly up to the top standards. We visited as often as we could, and took her away from there for brief visits with the family, too. We loved having her with us even though she had to be returned the home before the day ended, because she had to have her feeding tube tended and we had idea of how to operate or, care for it. So, though we didn't like it she had to be taken back.

There were more folks around the city who was sad and missed her beautiful singing voice and the music she could produce. She played for us at home, her home church choir and choirs in and around, Dallas. She had also been the music director for some of those churches since she was such a gifted pianist/organist.

Her ear for music was spectacular. Whatever song she heard almost, she was able to play! She could play the piano, the organ and even the guitar a bit. The fact that she could sing just made her a real joy to have in a church choir.

She had also lived in Los Angeles for a time, just as Elouise and Willie C. Even though Evelyn was there, neither Lean, Elouise or Willie C. chose to stay in California very long. They all returned back to Dallas. To all of them it was the place they called home.

Her not being able to talk to us except in signs and sounds was sometimes frustrating for her and us. We missed her vibrant spirit. We had no idea how long she would be ill or if she would get well, we were all hoping she would get better.

While all this was going on I was getting ready to retire, but on the way to that I was given a surprise.

I had spent 31 years in the classroom.

Bobby had retired in 1991, and his frequently telling of the things he was doing while I had to spend the day working encouraged my desire to join him in retirement.

I was nominated and by the teachers at Sam Houston Elementary School to be their Teacher of the Year. I was then put into the running for the Teacher of the Year for the district. I was the 1st Runner up as the Teacher of the Year for the Port Arthur Independent School District! Mr. Fred Mitchell, member of the PAISD School Board at the time gave me the plaque. I received that honor in April of 1993.

I had however, kept on course with my retirement idea. I was a bit surprised that my thing about wearing hats had gotten all the way to the administration building. The Superintendent of Schools referred to me as the "Hat Lady" during the ceremony. (I had made the decision to a wear a hat all the time several years before because of what one of my students told his mother about me.) At the time I was into wearing hats. Not just on Sundays, I had been doing that since I was able to do so after I got grown but, during this time I always had one on if, I left my house to go somewhere. The only time I

didn't wear one was when I was in my classroom teaching or singing in the choir. Well the Superintendent introduced me that way when I was given my retirement plaque.

A couple of family friends received their plaque at the same time, we even took a picture together, Levi Adams a vice principal and our neighbor and Rev. Raymond Cyprein, who had worked with Bobby and me at one time or the other. His last assignment was at Sam Houston with me. We were all very relieved to be set loose.

Lean was still in the home where she had had to be placed. When I saw her and told her of my retirement the only way she indicated that she knew what I said was through her smile. She hadn't been doing much smiling by this time though. She had a down turn a little while after I talked to her. She didn't get any better from the down turn of her health. She passed away July 20, 1993. Her passing was a tragic loss to our family!

We had a time realizing that our baby sister had gone to glory, but Mama's stanch reliance on the Lord helped us all. However it was a trying time for the family.

Then in the very next year Ausie got ill. This brother had spent some times here and there, in more than one state. He, like our next brother, Carlton was guilty of a few wild things in his life. He went crossed many, many miles from where we were reared and, engaged in some activities he would not wanted to write home about. His, were just not quite as wild as our brother Carlton's sometimes were, that we knew about.

Ausie brought one of his "Lady friends" to a family reunion. I use the term Lady loosely, she didn't seem to be as old as his children!

Ausie with one or his "friend"

I don't remember his being seriously ill but a few times in his life, but this time he was seriously ill. He had to be put on life supports! He was on them for a while, yet his health came to the point where the doctor informed the family that there was no reason to keep the life supports machines going. He was brain dead!

That was one heart breaking message the doctor had to give the family. No one really knows what that is like unless you have been in those shoes. Very few people want to play God at a time like that.

Someone had to make the decision of whether to turn off the supports or not. I was so very glad it was not my decision to have to make. His children and family members were the ones to do that. He passed away on February 23, 1994.

It was an even more heart wrenching time since it had not been, all that long a time since we had lost Lean. In my head I know God does things in HIS own way, on His own time, but it was just so hard. We made it with the help of the good Lord.

Later that year I had a very traumatic occurrence in my own life. I went to my family doctor for a **scheduled** visit, yet I had a number of things planned that I wanted to do that day after my visit with the doctor was over. But when I got there I was feeling rather weird. By the time I walked into her office I must have been looking a bit out of it, because she asked about how I was feeling. I described all the sensations I was having. She looked at me closely, then examined me listened to my and heart. She then called for a wheel chair and had me rushed into the walkway to the hospital across the street! She told me she felt that I needed to be in a hospital right then!

She ordered a number of tests to be done after having me checked into the Park Place Hospital. She also gave me some medication. It made me feel rather sleepy. I thank God I was because, what she told me would have been more than a bit alarming had I been fully myself. After going through the tests she had had done, she then told me that I needed major surgery. Some of my arteries seemed to be blocked. She suggested that I go to a doctor she had worked with in Houston. He was one of the ones who had worked with the heart doctor who had done several successful heart transplants there.

My husband and I selected to go there and let him do the surgery. I stayed in that Park Place only a day or two before being transferred to St Luke's Hospital in the Medical Center of Houston by ambulance!

Once I got there, I was examined by the doctor who tried to explain to me what he was going to do. He was very nice and seemed patient. After having tried to talk to me about the procedure, he even provided a video for me to look at, that would give me a more detailed account of the procedure I was to undergo. I went to sleep after only about a minute into the showing (for that I thank God) I didn't want or need to see it.

The surgery was done. It was then that I had the opportunity to find out what it was like to wake up feeling like part of my own body didn't belong to me! I also felt that there was a part of my life missing as well as feeling like the chest I had was not mine. It also felt like it weighed a ton! Just talking, could wear me out. They got me up and I walked a bit soon it seemed to me. Not too long after that they thought I was well enough to be released from the hospital.

It took months for my chest to feel like belonged to me. There seemed to be a rod down the middle of my chest that did not go away for awhile. It finally did though! After that, I just had a "zipper" down my chest. (Zipper, is what some of us who have that scar placed on our bodies call it) Along the length of the zipper, is where they had put those staples to hold my ribs and chest together so I could heal up from where the doctors had to open me up to open up the clogged arteries. They had had to slit open my ribs in that process. They used veins from my breast and my thigh to get the veins to put in place of the removed clogged arteries connected to my heart. It was what they called a Triple Bypass, which means I had three clogged arteries taken out and they had to take veins from around one of my breasts and my left thigh. This meant that other parts of the body was involved in the surgery and needed to heal as well.

I had one dear precious friend who understood what I needed most, her presence!

I believe Ola R. Pace somehow knew that talking was a real effort. She was the wife of my husband's fraternity brother (Sylvester Pace), fellow church member we were also both members of the mission and the Deaconess Board of the church. She would talk to me when I felt like it and when I needed to rest she would say, "Honey, you don't have to talk. I'll be here with you for awhile, just rest a minute or until you feel like talking."

When she came to visit she would bring a book, or something to keep her attention for a bit while I rested, or she would ask if the television was a bother. After I had had a bit of a rest then we would talk again. I loved her dearly!

In a few months I was back to going and doing much of what I had always done except teaching, since I had retired. Then it was full steam ahead!

Life got back to normal as if there had not been that set back.

Mama

One Memorable Trip to Memphis, Tennessee

I began going with the family member to the Convocations in Memphis, Tennessee the year I retired from my teaching job. I was ready to go back as soon as I had a chance, I enjoyed it so much. So I was ready to go back as soon as I had a chance.

It was thrilling for me. Especially since I got to go to some places I had only heard or read of like, the place where Dr. Martin Luther King got killed and, the Pyramid, as well as other well known places in and on the way to Memphis. There were a few not so well known places that e got to see.

These trips gave me a chance to be with Mama as she traveled and see for myself how much she enjoyed them. We were also able to visit the church of one of my favorite television pastors and stay for morning service! He died a few years ago and I still miss his thought provoking sermons.

On one of those trips to Memphis I had reason beyond measure, to thank God for He demonstrated for me and others that, He still works miracles. He performed one for us on our way there. As we always did, we traveled in cars. There were so many of us that we were in three cars, we were the middle car, and my sister was taking her turn at driving. We were on the Interstate 30 from Dallas to Memphis. This road was very busy it seemed to me, it was the busiest roadway I had ever traveled. This day it was as it usually is when I have gotten a chance to travel on it. It seems like **the** expressway for large trucks!

Our Brother was driving a few cars ahead of us and the other car that had been behind us had also driven ahead. There was a puddle of water on the lane we were in. When she hit it the car went in a circular kind of spin and slide onto the edge of the road and partway into the ditch. Mama, one of my other sisters and I were in the back seat At first I nearly lost it but, all of a sudden it seemed as if someone touched me on the shoulder, and said, "Don't lose it everything will be just Fine!"

Even though the slide/spin only lasted a little time, it seemed to have slowed down and the peace I felt was so comforting! Within the next few second my sister was on the road again, going in the right direction without even stopping! The rest of the traffic didn't seem to pause either. We all were so amazed and could hardly believe what had happened!

When we got to the next stop, we asked Zip, our brother who was just ahead of us and those with him if they had seen what had happened to us. Not one of them, in either car had! It seemed so unusual because the traffic was really thick. However what amazed us was that we did not even have to stop. We were just able to flow right on back into the stream of traffic going our way.

I am sure one can imagine that we had a marvelous trip! The stay in Memphis for the Convocation of the Church of God in Christ after that miracle was just great. We had a miracle on the way and a very blessed time after we got there. It was one experience that I have had tucked away into my memory stash since that time.

I continued going to those meetings with Mama and My sisters for years even after that until my sister Georgia who would be on the programs almost each time we went. She was there to help with the services; the rest of us just went for the enjoyment and enlightenment we received. That is why I think the trips continued until Georgia felt she was called into the ministry by God. She started her own church there in Dallas, Texas.

Nit and Sis

My Dear In-laws are taken

During the nineties the sad things were happening on the biological side of the family were not the only ones, there were other sad things on my husband's side of the family that affected me too. The strength of Mama's teaching and her life example helped me through those trying years.

We helped them celebrate their fiftieth wedding anniversary at the Butler Community Center.

Nit and Sis repeating vows

My husband did a poem of mine to express their loving tribute for their love sacrifices, sleepless nights, worry concerns, encouragements, needed chastisements, support, both financial, and moral, kind words of cheer and pride you both have offered unstintingly over the years to each of the children.

> You made our worlds beautiful with just the right things
> With a word you speak and the joy it brings
> You have given so selflessly time and time again
> Your love, concern and encouragements without end
> The gratitude felt within our hearts evades the simple words
> But it fills our souls with a glow and with a yearning that struggles to be heard
> Your many deeds of kindness like the dawn at the break of day
> Helped to fill our hearts with beauty and sped us on our way
> For fifty years your obligation to marriage and family you have successfully met
> And for your children, a worthwhile example you have set.
> If anyone of us should from our obligation stray
> It will *not* be because you, our parents, did not show us the way
> For every one of us you have always been there
> To express in every possible way, how very much you care
> Eight of the ten of us you sent away to college
> At this time, for all of us, I publically our thanks, acknowledge.
> Among us are, 2 principals, 3 teachers, and a registered nurse
> A fireman, cab driver and furniture specialist, we could certainly have been worse.

It was about this time that the family decided to build a new home for the parents. It was a home on par with our homes. It was a three bedroom, two bath brick home with a place for his pickup truck. It had most of the amenities that ours has, just in the country.

My Mother-in-law's health had begun declining. She had to be taken to the hospital more than once, yet her attitude was as nice as it had always been. But her condition caused her to have to spend with a while her daughter, Lela, in Dallas. For her that was really different. She was finally able to return home, but after going her health was never was the same. She was unable to do many of the things that she had always done. This had a real effect on the visitors she saw and her being there for so many in the surrounding communities. She even had to have a care giver for a while.

The Durham home on the corner of highway 84 and farm to market road 489 had been the place for people to stop on the way to town, when they came to the crossroad grocery store to just stop in for a chat, just to rest, or on the way to visit other people in the surrounding communities. They stopped to visit with her in her home.

She was the kind of person who made a difference in people's lives. To use the words of her daughter, LaWanda Durham Mitchell, "Sis did what she knew how, she really served. She had a generous sharing spirit. Her home on the corner allowed her many opportunities to share her friendly hospitality to brighten the day for those she encountered. Though of modest means, she exhibited a genuine art for living well."

She continued to weaken, then, she had to return to the hospital in Fairfield. She even had to spend a bit of time in one the nursing facilities there. Yet, on Monday, April 24, 1995, Ovena "Sis" Simmons Durham my dear mother-in-law ended her finite time on this earth. We lost her!

Since Sis was like a second mother to me, and had been for so many years I was really pierced to the heart. I know my husband's family was even more affected, too. All of our lives were suffering the loss of this dear loving person. The community was feeling it as well since she had been such a well known presence.

None of us suffered as much of a loss as Nit, her husband of more than 60 years! He had to remain in the home where she, had been the magnet that drew people, for so many years. People all around knew him, but when they would come to the house he was usually just a listener who would add a word or two every once in awhile, Sis would be the instigator of most of their conversations and the visits and great food many got there. He did fairly well for only a while, but then his health began to go downhill.

Bobby had started going home a bit more often after he retired. He had been taking both parents for their doctor's appointments even before Sis passed away. He continued to do that for his dad after she was gone. He also helped him find and buy a new pickup truck. He would take Nit to shop for groceries many times when he was there, even going by *The Sam's* very popular buffet restaurant in Fairfield where he always wanted a hamburger.

Bobby became worried after a time because his father would many times want to know from him, where Sis had gone. He was even putting a little money aside for her at the house for when he thought she would come back!

When he would tell him she had passed away, he would make some comment that meant that he already knew that.

During his lifetime Nit had worked the farm, and as a help for his family when that was not enough, he also worked for many of the people who had land or vacation homes on the lake not too far from his home. He also did a bit of carpentry work in the community as well. After he lost his wife his health also began to deteriorate at a rate we all thought was fast. He was not able to do too many of the things he had always done. Some of it might have had to do with his health. Some of it may have been due to his loneliness and some, the missing his of his wife, one as I stated before, had been with him for more than sixty years!

He was able to remain at home however, until he got into his new truck one day, drove several counties away from his home. He ran out of gas, he had no idea where he was or how to get back home. Some folks saw him and spoke because they knew him, and after talking to him, realized that he was completely lost. They called one of his sons to come for him. He was disoriented and had no idea where he was!

We were all completely shocked and, terribly worried about his physical and, mental condition. He had to be put in the hospital for a while. After his dismissal he was unable to go back home by himself, he then became a resident at the Manor Care Professional Health Care Center in Dallas. He was placed there because it was closer to his daughters. They felt he would be better there because of the nearness to them and they could visit more often. He was not able to go back home. He remained there until his death on Friday, December 11, 1998. His departure was another trememdous loss for the family.

The year or 1998 was a doubly sad on for me. I lost my loving father-in-law and my dear friend Ola Pace passed away!

I knew she was ill, so I visited her as she done for me times before. In her case as I had been, many times she could not communicate. That was no stumbling block to me, I just had the opportunity to do for her what she had done for me. Be there for her.

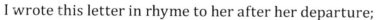

I just didn't get it for some time, why my heartfelt prayers for her were not answered the way I wanted them to be! I had to get closer to God for me to realize it was His will not mine that was in force.

I wrote this letter in rhyme to her after her departure;

My Dear Ola,

Right now it's hard for me to accept that you've gone to a better place
Maybe it's because we can't continue to see your slightly smiling face
*But, we must assure ourselves that, The **One** you're with is perfectly alright*
You were very dear and precious in His sight.
We are mourning; it takes time for God's message to get through
While Jesus was in human form, He cried for His friend Lazarus when he died too
Ola, we know your God given tasks are complete; your robe has been unfurled
Your suffering is over down here in this sinful world
Being ladylike, quiet, introspective and diligent was always you way
So many times your softly spoken ideas for us would save the day
You were a loving faithful, wife, mother, teacher Quette, deaconess and dear friend
Your labors, so steadfast and honest that we remember are now at an end
From beginning of our church, especially, you gave an important helping hand
You were not an idle talker but, you spoke up when need made its demand
The ladies' lounge in the church was once an empty place
Until a donation from you filled that empty space
The special appreciation service for our deacons, you encouraged us to institute
Is still quite unique, no one, even now, can dispute
You made an impact on so many, in so many ways
To relate the how's and who's could take and days and days

Take the numerous times that by illness I was laid low
Your caring visits would always comfort me so
No one else's company was as restful and relaxing to me
As the time when you my sister, me, would come to see
You were the kind of confidant in whom one could put their trust
For whatever I, told you in confidence, was always just between us
Like Dorcas/Tabitha, the woman Peter raised in Bible days
We, your friends will miss you so, because of your pleasing ways
We thank God for loan of you for this little while
We realize. The other day He sent an angel to get His tired faithful child
Your sojourn here enlivened and blessed our lives so much
We will always miss your presence and your special unique touch
We just thank God for sending you our way
Now, servant of God, we bid you His speed today!

These words of praise I had the opportunity to express at her home going service.

Life went along as usual for the next few years, but in the year 2002 my husband and I became grandparents for the first time!

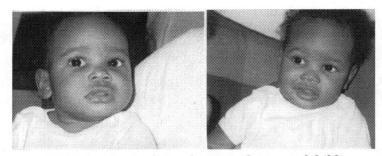

Little Shayna Nicole Durham our first grandchild!

The year for us was a year that was a very memorable one. It started out just as many others had, except my husband was honored at our church. He was personally thanked in the form of a special program, for all the work he does. He is one of the church's deacons, the Superintendent of the Sunday School as well as the treasurer of the church. The program was planned as a surprise for him. But since the boys and their significant others were invited along with members of his family he figured it out before he go to the church and the program actually got started. I was after that program that Ken and his wife gave us the news.

We had been waiting it seemed like, the longest time, but our sons had not produced any grands that we knew of.

Then Shayna!

Carlton

Carlton Says So-long

After Ausie went away before Daddy died, the oldest brother we had at home was Carlton. He was one of a kind! There were times he was a joy to have around then there were times one wondered whether he had it all together. Some of the antics he pulled were sometimes shocking, sometimes funny and at other times, as was stated before, "Off the chart".

He even went back East to stay, for no legitimate reason that any of the family could think of. He stayed for a while. I have no idea what he did there, but one day I got word from him that he wanted me to send money to him. He was ready to come back to Dallas, Texas and he was broke, I, was to send money for the fare to get home, to him!

After fussing, talking to Mama, my husband and some other family members, I sent it. It might have been terrible of me but, I stipulated that as soon as he got on his feet again he was to pay me back. He did.

His unusual behavior at times did not diminish after that wild trip. He was one of Mama's children that did not follow her example and become a believer, an acknowledge believer in God who attended church consistently. (One who wanted to live as God would have one to live.) He always wanted to do his own thing. I feel that it started to go so badly when Cotis fell out of the boat while they were fishing together, and died because he never seemed to be in control of himself after that. I have often wondered if he somehow felt responsible, even though we all believe he had a heart attack and that was the reason he stood up before falling into the water.

We, as a family had only a couple of years without being hit closely by death again but, Carlton, our wayward brother became seriously ill. There were a few things that were confusing that we had to handle after he was first placed in the hospital, one was who was to be responsible, and then he had to be placed in a nursing facility. At the place where he stayed his health went pretty fair for a while, then it went downhill.

Even while he was there his wife Rubye Fay did what she could to care for him, in spite of some of the wild things he had done. She visited him gave him things he needed. She even tried to provide for him when she found out he had no burial insurance. She was there for him until his death. He passed away February 14, 2003 after being taken back to Carlton Methodist Hospital there in Dallas.

This was another blow to the family but we carried on.

Mama and Me

We Face Other Challenges

The rest of that year passed away with me being as busy as I usually was. I was involved in community projects. In trying to fulfill my tasks as a chairman of the Citizens Drug Task Force for the city, officer in my church's district association, president of the church's missionary society and other offices at the church, working with the retired school personnel group, my sorority and visiting nursing homes and the sick in the area usually took up a bit of time. At least one full week in each month was back to back meetings or activities.

I let that busy schedule make Bobby and me late in evacuating before the hurricane that had come through our area the year before was to make landfall. It had taken us about two hours to go just seventeen miles from home, and another three hours to go about forty five or fifty more! So, at the onset of the 2004's hurricane season we decided that we were going to be ready to be on the move as soon as a notice was given. If we had to leave we would do it early. We did have to leave, evacuation was called. We were true to our earlier agreement we went as soon as the first notice was given!

As we had done on so many occasions before when we were asked to leave, we went home. Bobby's parent's home was as well equipped as our own. The only complaint I had was that the TV we watched did not carry the channels I wanted. At home we have cable. There they have a Dish. That was alright, except, there was **one** station that I wanted to see that was not part of that network. (Talk about reasons to complain, I was a very ungrateful soul considering what so many were having to go through at the time.)

We finally got the word one night that everything was calm on the Gulf Coast, those of us who had evacuated from there could return. We got up the next morning all packed and ready to go. I started to get breakfast and began feeling sick to my stomach. It was such that Bobby told me to sit down and he finished it himself. After breakfast we got in the car and started on our way home. We had only gotten about sixty miles away when I started to actually vomit. I would get out of the car on the first few times, then it got to be so fast that by the time we would stop, I would just opened the car door and lean my head out and put it out the door.

I was feeling so ill, as we drove along that the only way I could only keep myself together was by repeating scriptures that I could remember. We trying to get home, Bobby was driving a while and stopping for me to vomit out the door, for many miles. After traveling this way for more than a hundred miles I was feeling not only sick I felt filthy, when we got to Woodville. I felt I needed to get to a restroom and wash up. I had a feeling I was going to upchuck again so I just stuck my head out at first, as my husband pulled up onto a parking space at the Woodville Inn. Then as I was trying to get myself out of the car, a woman drove up. She noticed that I was having difficulties.

She came over, "Ma'am what is the problem? You look mighty weak."

"I am trying to get to the restroom. I've been vomiting for hours and I need to wash up a bit."

"Ma'am I don't think you are strong enough to even get to that hotel."

She looked over and told Bobby, "Mister you need to get your wife to a doctor as soon as possible!"

She helped me sit up and closed the car door and Bobby drove off. He drove the remaining miles to the doctor's office in Nederland. At this time I found out that I couldn't get out on my own. Bobby got help to get me out of the car, but he talked to the doctor. She looked at me, and called an ambulance immediately, that took me straight to the hospital!

There, they put me in emergency for a while, then sent me to a room. I found out later that I had had a major stroke on my right side. I had had a, I guess most will say a minor stroke, something they say it starts with an A but I can't pronounce , let alone spell, years earlier while I was still teaching. It had only affected my thumb with a kind of numbness. This time, I was weak on that right side. I was told this one was probably effect me for life. I was always sure in my own mind that I'd able to get back to my old self. I had the belief all along that I would be completely normal. Someone even told me while I was still in bed, "There are many folk who have watched you walk and read in the mall, but because of this stroke you probably won't be able see you do that again."

I never gave up the belief that I would.

I had a bit of therapy in Saint Mary's Hospital where I was but, was later moved across town to another unit in what was then part of Park Place Hospital. I was there for a while when I improved enough that I was on my way to walking completely normally by the time I was dismissed. I continued doing the therapy they did with me in the hospital once I came home. This was during the month of October, by the last of November I was walking as I usually did.

By the end of December I met the person who had told me that I would probably not be able to do my walking in the mall reading, at one of the doors to the mall as I was passing it during my usual walk around the mall! By this time I was back to doing my usual stuff, walking and reading with God's help.

One of the things I always did for Mama was getting things for her when I could, for her birthday, Christmas, Mother's Day and any other gift giving time I always bought her a dress or two. She loved it, and it was a way for me to know exactly what to get for those gift giving times. I had been able to even manage that for the Christmas time. That I was so pleased about.

I had spent many of my visits to Dallas after my retirement taking Mama to her doctor's appointments. Laura was working in her shops and was usually only off on Mondays. I didn't have to report to a job so I agreed to take her. At first she went to an extension of one of the medical colleges for the seniors or older persons. They were so really nice to the older people going there. This experience had led me to seek a female family doctor for myself after my family doctor had decided to retire years earlier. I found it so much easier to relate to a woman when I went with her.

Since her health was seemingly much better than mine after my illnesses, I didn't continue to go and take her to the doctor, especially because of my full schedule here at home in spite of my state of said retirement. It seemed all I was involved in so many things and it seemed to grow all the time.

It was somewhere along the way that I noticed that when I was with Mama and we ate, Mama would chew completely only a little of her food. She would chew then spit out the so much of it, unless it was of the very soft variety of foods like macaroni, mashed potato, and bread and there were times when she would just taste the food, then spit it out. This started at first when Mama had lost the bottom row of dentures because she would take them out of her mouth at times put them in a handkerchief, or paper napkin, I feel it was because they didn't fit properly. I took her to a place and she got another one. She kept up with it for a year or two. She then lost them again and mentioned it to me because I noticed that she was having trouble eating certain foods again so I talked to Laura about it and she said she had noticed the same thing. But she said that she would just loose them again. Besides she was getting to where she could eat more foods without it.

After a while we were all concerned when she started to do the gumming thing all over again only this time she was doing it even more. She wasn't eating much of *anything* that was solid. Laura took her to the doctor, but they didn't really tell her anything that was helpful. She continued to do this then she was taken to other doctors to find out what the problem was. We were given several possibilities. Yet nothing was done. It was within probably about the middle or last of 2006 that one doctor said that there might have been a problem with her stomach. More than anything we were told, **"She's doing well for someone at her age!"**

I had remembered an older deacon at our church who had gotten so aggravated with a doctor he was seeing because kept telling him the same thing. He, changed doctors. He got some more satisfying answers to his questions afterwards. I told Laura about it.

She also took Mama to see other doctors. There were times they even had to take Mama to the hospital a time or two, because at times after eating she would double over after eating almost anything, as if she was having severe pains in her stomach. She would only mourn and hum a bit because she didn't talk too much about how it felt, so we could not tell what she was feeling.

One of the things that she did stop doing was reading her Bible all the time she would be sitting and knock on the handle of her chair in the house! This I noticed and I bought her tapes of someone reading the Bible. She was not able to listen to it often because I don't believe she really knew how to operate the machine to play them. It was only after the many different bouts not eating and the pain in the stomach that Mama began to look more like an older woman.

Mama

After she had been suffering for a while one doctor finally had them take x-rays of her stomach. They then said she had some growths or nodules in her stomach. She was not eating very much of the foods she put on her plate. Mama's stomach pains got to where she was only able to consume 'ENSURE,' the liquid drink they give to folks who get to where solid foods are a problem. Many times she could still eat a few foods with the consistency of baby food, yet we were still bothered that we did not know what exactly what her problem was especially, since she was getting weaker.

During September of the year of 2006 I went to a birthday celebration for the mother of one of my friends who goes to church with me. She was just about six or seven months younger than Mama. It was really nice. Her mother who, before and after the celebration, was in a much weaker shape than Mama was. She seemed to have enjoyed the event so much that I made the decision then, that I was going to get my family together for an occasion like that if she made it to her next birthday. For the first time in my life I was wondering about Mama's life expectancy, and I wanted give her a special kind of birthday celebration like that one.

I started making doing what I could to set it up the very next time I talked to the other members of the family. I call all the members of the family every weekend anyway, so when I talked to them I mentioned the celebration. They were all in favor of it so I started planning. One of my nieces, Angie helped me with the things that needed to be typed and a few other things. My sister Georgia told us we could use her church for the celebration. Some of us decided we would furnish food for the occasion, and Vicki, Luke Junior's wife, decided to decorate the cafeteria of the church where we were to eat.

For the special day I decided to get Mama a special outfit for the occasion. I found one here in Port Arthur. The whole outfit was in gold. She was seated at the front of the church in a very elaborate chair with lions on each side of her. She was a little surprised since she usually had her special seat at the church and it was not up front!

On the day of the celebration all the members of the family were showed up. She was so very pleased and so was I. We had a full program planned.

Luke and Mama at her birthday celebration

The program went well, Mama and all the family seemed to have enjoyed the program
And the time we were all together.

Later Mama became ill and had to be taken to the hospital, again. While she was at the hospital they even suggested that Mama be put on Hospice Care! This was very traumatic for all of us. It seemed to us that this was the doctor's way of saying, "She is **not** going to get better. We have given up any hope that she will ever get well. We feel she ought to be allowed to die".

We were not nearly ready for something like that! The family took her out of the hospital as soon as they could and she was treated at Laura's home for some time. She seemed to get better; she even went back to church and visiting members of the family.

By January of 2008 Mama's health was consistently worse than it had ever been. She was not out of bed or even sitting up very much that I knew about. Though we were a bit worried ourselves we could not figure out what else we could do. Her condition was at a point where I was asking my own doctor for suggestions about what to do for her to make her feel better and she had not even met her! Some of her suggestions helped for a while.

At this time I was trying to carry on as usual. I had even planned a trip on behalf of the committee that I am chairman of for the city, to a Texas Safe and Drug Free School Conference in Corpus Christi. The day before I was to leave I got a call telling me Mama had passed away!

In spite of the fact that I knew she was not getting better even with all the things the family was trying to do. I still hoped with the prayers and all we were doing that she would get better and be her old self again. It was just that we were not ready to be without her presence in our lives.

After her death I tried to come to terms with her being gone, but it is still a real trial. Putting together this chronicle/record is one of the ways I thought would help me through the most difficult part. I am still suffering the loss of her smile, and her presence at Laura's when I go to Dallas. Mama's passing away is like a knife to my heart and I have a feeling that it is to my brothers and sisters, too.

How does one forget the strength she provided with her words of wisdom and her stabilizing presence? She was there for us all; at any and all times we needed her. She always made sure we knew that we could trust our loving God not only by telling us, she demonstrated with her life the things she did and how she lived!

The times I was a member of the Poet's Review in 1996 I wrote that expresses my sentiment even today:

All my adult life I have wondered if there would come a day
When a child of mine would come up to me and say
"Thank you Mother Dear for being so loving and true,
And doing all the things for me that Grandma did for you!"
That, for me would be the greatest compliment
'Cause you, my Dear Mama was the best God ever sent!

When God assigned my brothers, sister and me a mother, he picked the very best there was!

They all Remember Mama

Mama at 96 years

Family Members remember Mama

Mama touched the lives of all the Family not just me
She wanted us to be all that God meant for us to be
She had an influence on her children and the grands
Many of them got instructions and discipline from her heart and at her hands

This is the point where I decided to include the reflections of as many other family members as were willing to put their feeling on paper. They all had to get them to me, either by 'snail-mail' or email.

Most were a bit hesitant except Angie, my niece. She got her write-up in real early. The others came later and then later. Each person was very willing to add to the memories of her our wonderful mother.

Mama's Children and Grandchildren

Otis Weaver

Ausie Jones   Evelyn Jones Rider

Cotis, Isiah, Uncle Luke, Carlton, Elouise, Mama, Eddie, Willie C, Georgia, Laura, Luke, Jr., and Venus Lean

Grands at family gathering at much young ages

Some more of the grand children at older ages

Rev. Otis Weaver

Son and child #1

"Mama's Oldest Child, the first Minister"

I was Mama's oldest child. Even though she left my father when I was only three years old and I was raised by my father, grandmother and grandfather I got to know my mother later in life and came to love her.

I was in fact about thirteen years old before I got to see my mother after she left me and my younger brother Cotis with our grandmother.

My brother Cotis (Son and child #2)

She was with her second husband Mr. Will Jones. He would bring Mama and the family to see us.

I even went to the school at Shiloh with my brothers and sisters because we grew in the same community!

When I was 17 years old I went to visit her on a Sunday. I promised that a few friends and I were going fishing. It was to be in an area where were to fish and just hang out together. But, we a different decision after we had been there for a while. There was a girl I had feelings for not too far away across the woods. Her name was Pauline. I decided I would go visit her instead because I was with a few friends who were, a bit wild, like me and they all were in favor of my going there.

After I got there I didn't come home when she suggested I get back. For that infraction she gave me a whipping that night! While she was doing it she was preaching me a brief sermon on good behavior and truthfulness. I wasn't as much hurt by the whipping as I was the sermon.

I was scheduled to go to the army the very next day! This was on a Monday, in 1945. The lesson she tried to teach me lasted. It stayed with me all through my term in the army. I was very diligent in staying within the rules after that. I am now 81 years old and I still remember it.

When she needed help after Mr. Will died Cotis and I went to bat for her because we kept up our relationship with her after we left the area and moved to Dallas. We took her to a doctor here in the Dallas area. Even thought she stayed with our aunt, we kept in touch took her to the hospital or doctor when needed.

I even remember taking her to a doctor that I wanted to give a piece of my mind because of a comment he made when we took her there to see him. He was a very good doctor so we took her back, I didn't particularly like him but, he helped Mama. So, we took her back.

In spite of the fact that I was not with her all my childhood, I loved my mother beyond measure.

Minnie Weaver

The Wife of Otis

The first time I met Mother Babe I saw that she was a spiritual, nice humble person. Every time I saw her she was the same person. She didn't change in all the years that I knew her.

I loved her very much because seemed more like a mother to me than a mother-in-law. I was always glad to see her. I just wish it had been so that I could have spent more time with Mother Babe. I will always love her although she has passed on.

I will remember Mother Babe as always being the same.

Elouise Jones

Daughter #1 and child #3

"Mama for Me"

My mother, Everlena Jones Durham, was a praying woman. She was sweet to everybody. She was nice to all people and a real lady. She did not talk about anybody in a bad way, because the Bible says that we are not to do so.

She was one who wanted to be obedient to what she felt the Bible taught a Christian and a submissive wife to be. She was a real worker for and in the church as a member of the church and missionary society.

I was the oldest and only girl for a long time. I had two older brothers and two other brothers after me.

Mama made all of my clothes. She wanted to make sure they were all just right. The skirts to the dresses were real full most of the time. I liked to swirl around in them. I thought they were so pretty.

As the oldest and only girl I had to wash the dishes. There were times that I would look and think there were too much silver, forks, spoons, knives. While I was doing the dishes I would put some of the utensils under the house to keep from having to wash them. When she caught me boy did I get in trouble!

She would take me to town on my birthday. It was a real treat, even though I didn't usually get much more than an apple I would have a wonderful time. I would be so glad and always looked forward to that special time.

I was seven when Mama began teaching me how to cook. I was doing it for the whole family and, I felt that if I didn't do it just right I would get in trouble. When I got a bit older she taught me how to make quilts especially during the winter when it was cold. I even learned to make pillowcases and sheets. I would embroider designs on then. They would be so pretty. I would also have to iron them when they were washed before we put them back on the beds.

Whether we had to go to the field or school every day, even after the other children were born, it was my job to get things ready for everybody. She was working all the time doing something like working in the garden, raising the chickens for the family to have food

She did her best to make sure we did only what was right. She taught us to love one another.

Even if people talked about us she would tell us to pray and let God would take care of it. We needed to always be a lady. She was always talking to me

Part of her teaching took place around the fire. There she read to us, recited poetry and read the Bible.

She also made sure we went to church not only on Sunday she took us had us in a row on Wednesday night as well on our way to God's House.

Mama talked to me so much. She warned me over and over not to "get big"/pregnant.

She told me that it would ruin my life. She wanted me to make something of myself, to be somebody. I didn't understand a lot of things about life. I was disobedient; I did, get pregnant before I got married. Mama was really broken hearted. She cried so very much.

She always tried to give me the things that would help me in life. She was so very nice to me in spite of everything, but I guess it was not enough, I had one baby her name is Mary.

Mary Ola

She didn't know what to say to me afterwards because people just talked about us. But all she did was prayer late at night until she clapped her hand and cried out, it would hurt me so bad to hear her. I for me was so difficult since my heart I felt that I could do nothing right. My self esteem was very low. I always thought people didn't like me. Mama would try and tell me good things. She tried teaching me things to help.

Then I had another child Vester Earl. After that I gave up on myself. Mama still prayed for me but, I still didn't know what to do. I had a family in my mother's house. I felt it was not good. My life went down. But, Mama continued to love me. Vester died.

At this point I was left alone. I went to school, and got to the 12th grade but, the officials wouldn't let me have my diploma. I cried so much. The little self esteem I had left was gone totally gone!

Mama told me that "The Lord would make a way."

I left home after getting married and living in west Texas for a "minute." By this time I had another son, Ralph. The marriage didn't last then, I moved my son and daughter to an apartment in the projects of West Dallas.

Mama would come there to see about me. She also never stopped praying for me. She lifted my name to the Lord along with all her children and grandchildren.

Mary was her oldest grandchild, she would go with the others to visit her Big Mama, and she shared her love with all her grandchildren like she did with her children all her life.

Mama and Elouise

Willie Clemmons Jones

Son #4 and Child #6

"Mama's Bad Boy"

Mama always tried to teach me to be a good person but somehow that is not what she always got. I really got into quite a few things, that were not to Mama's liking nor, were they of any good even in my own eyes. She always taught me to be a man. She always told me to do the right thing and to. "Do unto others as you want them to do to you" a rule taught in the Bible. I try to do this, even when I come short, it's not because she didn't tell me.

I was always getting into mischievous things, like the day I was messing with some of the other kids and I knew Mama was about to whip me. I was at the kitchen door and I took off. To let me know that I couldn't get away from her I took off. She threw the wash pan at me. It clipped me and I had sense enough to stop.

When I started smoking I didn't want her to know. To keep her from finding out about it, one time when I was home, she was coming out my way when I had my cigarette lit; I hid it under the corner of the house and went the other way. She went and got it and brought it to me and told me to take care of it because she knew it was mine.

After Joyce and I married we were visiting with my niece Mary and her husband and we, Mary's husband and I decided to go fishing at a place near our home called Larkin Dam. They didn't want to do that they said they were going to pick berries.

Mama made some of her delicious tasting smothered chicken. They ate all of it before we got back! And they hadn't even picked ay berries. When we got there they decided to go pick them. Clarence, the man who was cultivating the land next to the house, had just plowed the field. While they were going to where the berries were they saw a snake. That really upset them so they came screaming toward the house. Uncle said he would pick them if they were too scared. They decided to let Uncle Luke pick the berries

Near the time when she was to be taken from us and we would not see her for a while and came in to speak to her, we'd say, "How are you Mama?"

Her answer would be, "I'm jumping but, not high. I'm flapping but, I can't fly."

When she was really low sick and I made these remarks she would even recognize it was me in the room with her.

I am still working on being the kind of man she wanted me to be!

Lillie Joyce Smith Jones

"Willie C's Wife"

My memories of "Miss Babe" started when I visited her at her home in the country. She showed me such gracious hospitality while I was there. I certainly can remember her fixing me some very good tasting greens. She even picked wild greens we called 'pork sally' and mixed it with other greens, even her collard greens were so tasty! She did it all for me.

I remember her very good tasting teacakes. I also remember that when she would bake them while we visited her at home, she would give us all some to eat while were there. But, on many of those occasions if Luke Junior was there with us, he would get some there with us, *and* she would also give him a hidden bag full, to take home with him! He would be able to eat them for days after we left.

When she moved to Dallas to live with Laura and I was able to see her more often I would come in and speak to her and ask her how she was doing and she would answer with some kind of saying like, "I'm kicking, but not too high!" or some other of her favorite sayings. She had a lot of them.

I would find it riveting when she and Tone` were into it. He would yell, "Grandma is trying to hook me with her cane!" for some reason or another.

I loved 'Miss Babe' and I am convinced she loved me, too!

Evelyn Juanita Jones Rider

Daughter #2 and child #7

"This is How I Remember Mama"

I am Evelyn Juanita Jones Rider Mama's eighth child up and the seventh child from the top when you include Ausie. I remember Mama as a very quiet lady and a very loving mother. She would start breakfast very early. Not long after that she would start lunch. It seemed she would spend most of the day cooking. But she also found time for washing clothes, working in the garden and showing all of us love and compassion.

I was an outdoor child who would stay dirty most of the time. Mama did her best to make me a lady out of me, but I was busy outside taking care of and running with the animals.

I was about 8 or nine when I first noticed she was a praying woman. I remember hearing her prayers at night and even through the night. Some of them have stayed with me all of my life. I was taught through my teen year still remember her saying, "If you don't work, you don't eat. If you work you will be able to keep a roof over your head.'

These sayings have kept me all my life. To this point I have had a lot of tough times, but her words were with me wherever I was when things got bad. In my mind, she would be there to tell me that, "The Lord will provide."

I got married and went to California at the age of sixteen and a half, so I was not around her, in body, often through a lot of years. She was still with me through God, even through hard times, and as often as she could, which was not often, she would come in person to visit. We would have such a wonderful time.

Mama was a lady who loved to go, ice cream from Sonnets and singing.

A few years before her demise years ago I kept her while Laura was on vacation and she just walked out the door. She had said nothing to me. All of us who were still in the city were looking every place we could think of to find her. She had been gone so long we got the police involved in the search eve the street helicopters were in on the search.

Then, someone suggested that we go by Chuck E Cheese's. She had suggested that someone take her there after she had gone there for one of her grandchildren's birthday parties and no one had. When they got there and there she was!

When we talked to her about it she said a nice young man took her there. He had passed her after she left the house and got down the street, he asked where she was going.

She told him she wanted to get to Chuck E Cheese's. He took her there. When she got there they asked what she wanted she told them and they brought it!

She let anyone know that talked with her that she had a good time. The rest of us were almost going out of our minds, Laura was ready to come back home and she was sitting up at Chuck E Cheese!

About a year before her death I was leaving Laura's house and looked back and she was running after me really running, she want to go somewhere!

I really loved that lady! It has been really lonely without her!

Isaiah Jones (Wife Bessie)

Son #6 Child #8

"My Memory of Mother"

Mama was a woman saved and dedicated to God for Lord every as long as I can remember.

She also had strict rules that one was to live by. When I would leave home, I knew when I should return to be in line with the rules she had for us at home. Though I knew this, I didn't always do it. One time I can remember going out and didn't come home by sundown, as was the rule. She didn't jump me right away, waited until I had gone to sleep, then came in and pulled the covers back and gave me a whipping with no cover or clothes in the way to protect me even a little!

Even then, I never stayed home like I was supposed to do. She called me "a street-filled lizard." I would even hitch-hike and go everywhere I could during the summer.

Mama would tell me those 'chicks' you are messing with and the stuff I was going after, are going to sour in my stomach. She would tell me, it is better to say, "Yonder he goes, than to say here he lay."

I was the first one out of all of us to receive the Holy Ghost! It happened when I was in the eleventh grade sitting, in the back of the church at Owen Chapel Church of God in Christ. I spoke in tongues for half the night. Georgia said "If I have to get it like that I don't want it."

I moved to Dallas when I was nineteen years old after helping Mama with the farming that summer. Afterwards I told Mama I was moving.

I have been around Mama as she has gone the loss of two husbands, my daddy and Uncle Luke, and watched her stand tall each time because of her faith in God. I watched God give her every promise of being there/with her, until He called. She saw generation after generation come, up to five that she was able to see.

This gives me to know that God is not short on His promises, what He did for her He can also do for me her son. As it says in the word, "The seed of the righteous shall inherit the earth.

Mama planted and nurtured good seeds

Laura Lee Jones Goosby

Daughter#4 child#9

"Mother Spent Her Last Twenty-plus Years with Me"

This is a few reflections that come to my mind when I think of Mother. I was blessed to be the child to be around Mother more than the other children. I was privileged and honored to have been able spend so much time with her.

She was a very quiet, humble God fearing woman who loved God and her family. I remember seeing her sneak out to our outside toilet ('The Outhouse') crying because she was no financially able to pay for a pair of hose and a white dress for my graduation!

She spent her life making our house a home. My father died when I was very young, about seven years old. Mother spent her time working with her hands in the fields, sewing or wherever she could make a dollar to feed and take care of her children. We had no television only a battery operated radio. She became our actress, comedian, soloist and poet. She taught us the importance of going to church. Most of all she taught us how important it is, to get along with one another, what a blessing!

She made our clothing with material Uncle Luke brought from up at the Crossroad Grocery Store and the sacks that flour and meal used to come in. She used whatever she had to make her little dark-skinned children look the best that we could.

Mother was strong woman, as I watched her I was able to acquire and use that strength she exemplified before me. As I grew to be an adult, in every situation of my life her saying, "God will provide" and "God will make a way," has been my standby.

Mother loved to go. She could get dressed in a flash. But, once out when she was ready to go home she would let you know! It was one of Mother's traits my sister Elouise acquired from her. We used to travel every year to places like places in California, Las Vegas, Nevada, Memphis, Tennessee, and others for one convention or the other. She loved it.

Everlena 'Babe' Durham
Taken on one our many trips

Her favorite place to go in her nineties was to the Senior Citizens Day Care Center. She attended every day until she could not do it anymore because of her illness.

Some of Mother's favorite or phrases that she repeated so often in her later years were, "huka'-huka', forgit cha', forgot cha,' cause I never thought about cha'".

She would always tell my grandson Tone` as he was growing up and thinking of himself as grown, "You are not a man, but just the image of a man. A hungry man will eat whatever is put before him. But, you, you have an appetite that is so choosy!"

Tone` Jones

Mother loved to cook. She taught me how to can vegetables, make preserves, and make a meal when it seems like you have nothing in the refrigerator. She loved to make, for her family, her famous teacakes, one thing I didn't learn to make. She made them until she couldn't remember the ingredients.

In her later years, you could tell when she had made in an instant when you walked into the kitchen. There would be flour all over. It would be on the wall and the countertop. She would not stop with the teacakes though, she go on to do pork chops and sometimes would use powdered sugar thinking she had used flour.

That was when I really –really knew that her cooking days were over. It turned my husband James' appetite away from pork chops forever.

I am the beautician of the family, but Mother like coming to the beauty shop so she wore a wig. She thought she looked better wearing one, so she wore one even to bed! Near the end of her life, I had to bathe her, and even when she had bath she wanted her wig. I would tell her she looked like a princess.

Mother wearing one of her wigs

James Goosby

Laura's Husband and Mama's Helper

I am Mrs. Durham's son-in-law but I always felt as though she were my own mother. I spent lots of quality time with her, since she lived with my wife and family most of our married life. While my wife, Laura, dressed her every morning in her last days, I would prepare her breakfast and we would go off to the Center.

She would always say I was her "designated driver" and she would not get into anybody's car unless she could behind the driver. When I would pick her up I would always have to stop at Jack-in-the-Box. She wanted a Jumbo Jack hamburger, one of her favorite foods everyday!

If she was not ready to go home when we got there, she would not get out. Sometimes she would sit in the car for an hour or more.

I would leave it up to Laura to convince her to get out, which was not always an easy task It was really expedient many times because it may have been either too hot or too cold for her to remain there.

She had many friends at the Senior Citizen Center but one special friend would wait until she was being pushed to the car, when she was leaving, and stand in her path just to tell her, "Now you take it easy," before she left.

Mother had loved to cook and until she started to forget her seasonings. Once she cooked some pork chops and she mistakenly used powdered sugar for flour on the pork chops as breading!

I stopped eating pork chops, at that time, is when I knew it was time to take the knobs off the stove or whatever I needed to do to keep her from continuing her attempts at cooking!

It was a great joy just knowing Mother. I miss her very much!

Georgia Mae Jones Ellis

Daughter #5 child #10

My mother as I remember her was a very sweet, kind and very easy to entreat. She was one who could be touched by anyone. She was one who loved her family very, very much and did whatever it took to be there for all of them, no matter what.

She was a Godly, praying person. Many times I would miss her inside our home, she would have tipped outside and I would find her sitting on an old stove (One that had been taken outside the house and placed behind the plum trees out back) there, she would be talking to God in prayer.

She was not a woman who just prayed when things were going wrong, but she also prayed when things were just fine. She had a constant relationship with God. He was not just a savior to her He had become her Lord. He was not someone/something she just believed in, she got to **know** Him.

Mother always believed in the power of prayer. She convinced me that prayer would work in any situation. Praying in the spirit always, no matter what lip could offer she taught me that you can **always** depend on God, trusting that whatever crisis one is in God is there. She had an anchor in God against all odds.

I think of my mother and I get tears in my eyes, not just because of the sadness of missing her myself, but of her not being here anymore to demonstrate for all of us the courageous and God fearing person she was.

After our father died she had to take up the role of trying to be both mother, and father knowing that tough times don't last but tough, strong people who have God on her side do. Nothing shook her confidence or her faith in God.

Mama's life brings to mind several women of the Bible as I think of her life and all that she did to influence my life and others.

The first one to come to mind is Rahab in the book of Joshua 2; 6:17-25. She hung a scarlet cord of prayer from the window. This was done to save her house. Mama may have used another method but she trusted that her actions would save her family.

Then there was her representation of Hannah (1Samuel 1) who wouldn't let go of prayer until she gave birth to whatever it was she wanted God's hands to provide. She was also a model of Sheba (1Kings 10) who was looking for wisdom in making decisions. She was the embodiment of a woman like Anna, (Luke 2) who was with Simeon at the temple when he met Jesus that was not destroyed by a broken heart! She was to us a Dorcas (Acts 9) as she took flour sacks and created beautiful clothes for my sisters and me. We looked rather pretty in the clothes she had made with her own hands. As the Shunamite woman (2 Kings) she had to be a creative thinker. She became an Esther (Esther) who would risk her life for her little children and family. At all times she displayed the traits of Lydia (Acts 16) who always gave God first place in her heart no challenge was too great with the help of God. As were Sarah (Genesis) she was my princess and will be honored by all who got know her children.

She taught by example know and watch her life was exciting and enriching!

I remember when we had no television, she became our entertainer. She would recite poems she knew or create ones of her own to capture our attention. This would keep us from fighting and fussing as siblings do. It would keep us focused on her until bedtime. I would go to sleep thinking, "When I grow up to be an adult, I am going to be just like my Mom." (Guess what, I am the one with the most children in the family)

She was a great Bible teacher. She taught Sunday school and read her Bible aloud around the family or whoever was there when she was reading. I'd listen to her and think, "I want to be just like that when I grow up." She put the desire into my spirit to want to be a teacher.

Many times I didn't understand why she would not allow us, to go to a lot of the places that other parents allowed their children to go to. On top of that she would warn us if she did let us go, that we had to be home before dark/sunset!

Now I have come to know that it was for our good. She seemed to know as a mother of what God used Moses to teach the Israelites/world what the parents need to pass on to their children to help them get to know that God is there all the time.

She was a mother who never just sent her children to church, she was there with us.

As I look back on her declining years while she lived with my sister, Laura the things would say and do was sometimes startling and at times very funny. She could be very real and funny, too.

I can remember a time when she was keeping my granddaughter, Andrea; all the grandchildren knew that Granny would get them for getting into mischief. She told Andrea she had done something that earned her a whipping. She said "I am going to get you!" She then went out to get a switch. While she was out Andrea locked the door and wouldn't let her back inside. She looked at her and teased her through the window saying things like, "Wow, Great Granny you can't get back in!" All the family **knows** that when Granny did get back in, it was ON in camp!

We had a few things that happened during her declining years that brings smiles even today and others that make for some heart wrenching moments even in memory

I remember during the summer 2001 my sister Laura and family went on vacation and left her with another sister. She did not like the fact that she did not get to go. While she was gone, Mama decided she would run away!

She did. We searched for her along with Dallas police for more than four hours after we found she was gone and not with any of the other family members. She was found in **Chuck E Cheese's** sipping a coke!

When she saw us coming toward her, asking about where she had been, letting her know how worried we were wondering where she was, along with other statements. Her comment to us was, "I knew you would come. I just wondered how long it would take you to find me." I was waiting for Cindy." (Cindy is my daughter would take her to **Chuck E Cheese's** from time to time.) She loved to watch Chuck E do a dance. She thought it was quite funny.

We would often laugh because when she was in church, during her later years and she was ready to leave, whether church was over or not, she would tell the person next to her, "Let's ride Clide!" or she would get Laura's key and leave from inside the church and sit outside until church was over.

Later I became the pastor of the newly formed church Deliverance Outreach Prayer Center and she attended there. On the times we would be gathered for service she and she wanted to leave before we were ready for dismissal, she would get ready to leave and would speak out, or tap on things noticeably. If that didn't work she would tell, whoever was listening, "Tell that girl to sit down. She can't tell it all in one day!"

She kept people around laughing.

Thanks to God for allowing her to be my mom. She was my princess and mentor.

Luke Durham, Junior

Last Child #14

My Sweet Mom

I was born on October 13, 1952 the last child of the family. The brothers and sisters that were at home by the time I started taking note of who was there Zip, Laura, Georgia and Lean. Our niece Carolyn was there for a while. We were very close because we were the same age.

Carolyn and I started school together and that same year Laura and Zip finished high school. Shortly after they finished Carolyn left for California to live with her mother, Evelyn.

In another year or so Georgia finished school. She left for Dallas and that left only Lean and me at home. Then in another couple of more years Lean also finished high school. I can't remember what year it was but Big Mama, our grandmother, came to live with us. Mama was there for her because our grandma had problems, too. Mama did all she could for her.

From the time I was very young, at different times grandchildren (my nieces and nephews) would come to stay with us. Mary, Ralph, 'Netta' (Bernetta), Linda (Berlinda), Terrance, 'Shan' (Chanellon), Clarence, Angie, Delaney, Diron Charles and Michelle are the ones that I remember being there at one time or the other. Mama kept so many of her grandchildren some for the summer some for years it didn't seem to matter. She was there for all of them.

In the spring and summer we worked in mother's garden and in the fields, where Dad had planted peas, corn and different crops because they were farmers. Whichever grands were there had to help too.

Mother loved to fish, some of the time we would go with Aunt Lula, Cousin Bessie Henry, Mrs. Metta Malone and some of the other women in the community. That is how I learned to fish. I enjoyed it. It didn't matter that I was the only boy with these ladies, Mama took me along and I had a good time. Mama didn't seem to mind having me along.

As I got older my job was mowing lawns. When I was in my teens I would go to Dallas for summer jobs or babysit as others went to work. Whatever money I made I would buy school clothes.

I finished school in May 1971 then moved to Dallas and went to work after having been there for a while I got married. We stayed married for a couple of years, we divorced then I joined the navy, following that the Navy. Then I joined the Navy Reserve for the next 20 years.

In the month of October, 1982 I got with my present wife, Vickie, she traveled with me to many of the places where I was stationed during those years I served. Mama seemed so proud of me while I served our country but was really relieved when I was finally completed my tour and was home and safe.

The most precious time that Mama spent with all of us I think was Reading the Bible and taking us to church. Sometimes we walked from Shiloh to Owens Chapel Church of God in Christ for service.

Mama was the best Christ-like person I have ever known in my entire life. Her mind stayed on God. She would always praying, singing or humming hymns. She was a woman of great faith. She taught us all to trust in God and to know that, "The Lord will provide." She had a listening ear, warm words of comfort a warm hug and a kiss on the cheeks. She would assure you that everything is going to be alright, if you just trust God!

Thanks to God, for a mother whose love never dies!

Vickie Durham

"Luke's Wife"

"A Letter to My Mother-in-Law"

To my Mother-in-Law

Mrs. Everlena Durham

I have been blessed with a mother- in- law that was truly God sent. Your loving care, have made me a better person and you have always been there for me. I have known you for twenty- five years and your personality and demeanor have been a great joy in my life.

There have been many days in my life where I have been sad, but your comforting love and support always inspire me to do my very best.

I remember the time we spent a weekend together and we shared stories that made us laugh. We talked about life trials and victories as well as my marriage to your son. Your words were "pray and hang in there". I know that no other person will have a beautiful mother-in-law as you

You are truly a virtuous woman and a woman of God.   No matter what has happen with me and your son, you have never turned your back on me and I thank you from the bottom of my heart. During your sickness you still showed me how much you love me.

I thank God for blessing you with a son that I have shared twenty-five   beautiful years with. Thank you mama and I thank God for creating you to be the woman that you are.

I love you with all my heart and I will never forget you.

Until we meet on the other side of Glory

Love always
Your daughter-in law
Vickie Durham

The Grandchildren Have a Say

Elouise, my mother

Mary Ola Brown

Mama'1st Grandchild

How I Remember Big Mama

I couldn't say I knew who Big Mama was I just know she was sent from God. I thought she could do, no wrong or think, wrong!

I knew if my Big Mama prayed all was right with the world. She prayed every night, mornings before breakfast, before lunch and for everyone she thought needed it. I remember when I was small always getting on my knees and praying before bedtime each night because Big Mama always did. I even remember saying some things that my mother, aunts, uncles and Big Mama found very funny while trying to imitate Big Mama praying a time or two. My family tells me this story I had seen a movie with Randolph Scott in it, so when I got on my knees and started to pray with Big Mama I started repeating out loud, "Oh Randolph Scott, Randolph Scott." That's who I thought she was saying/praying to and I wanted to pray out loud like she did.

I knew she smiled like the angel I thought her to be because I had the meanest great-grandmother on the planet! She was so different from my Big Mama. My great-grandmother was mad about everything. She said what she wanted to, to anyone she wanted to, especially to my Big Mama. I didn't like that but, Big Mama would attribute it to all her meanness to her being old and/or sick.

I didn't understand that either. One day Big Mama was changing her clothes and just to be terrible she messed in her 'undies' to make Big Mama have to clean her. She was always doing mean things like that to make Big Mama doing things for her, "Instead of those stupid babies (her Grand children). I was hurt when she said that.

When she died, I hurt for my Big Mama because she had to go through her old house to find money to bury her. I thought to myself, "She loved and took good care of her until she died."

Another reason I knew my Granny loved me was because one night we had gone out of town for my aunts, Georgia and Lean, to sing I think it was a meeting in Waco, Texas. When we got back I had to use the bath room, you had to go outside for that, and it was # 2. 'The Pot' was for #1 only, even at night. I did #2. She knew it was me but took it out and cleaned up the pot, I sunk so deep in the mattress, she said noting. I *knew* she loved me. This was one of the many times she showed her love to us.

I don't care what time Big Mama went to bed she was always up to make breakfast. It did not matter how many people were in the house she made all the food. Uncle Luke would be there at the head, yet Big Mama would always pray for the world! A prayer that took as long, as she wanted it to take.

I was ready to eat some of Big Mama's good food. She made the best fried chicken, biscuits and gravy get. You could love her just for that. Oh, and don't leave out the teacakes!

I remember going to school one time with my aunts, Georgia and Lean I got on the big bus with them, I went to the big wooden school with the big rooms and windows. I thought I was a big girl. I was supposed to go home with my Aunt Frances, on my dad's side of the family. I didn't think they liked me. This was when I was very young and I cried and cried but Lean and Georgia had to let me go.

I was so scared and it was a long walk to their house. They lived in what to me, were the back woods. It even seemed so dark. The house was real big, with a big porch and lots of big dogs. My grandfather only had to say one thing to them and they would obey. Even so, I was still scared.

Their house compared to Big Mama's house seemed big and dark with so many big rooms. The inside was never was the same way my Big Mama's. I would have to stay overnight and I was so glad when morning came. I used to think *they* made yellow eggs. When I got older I didn't dislike going there nearly as much as I did when I was little, especially since I grew to like Grandma Metta's sweet pickles and beets. I was still happy to get back to Big Mama.

On night at Big Mama's house we; my Aunts Lean and Georgia and, my Uncle Zip and I were sitting on the front porch. They we talking about the light in the front, because when it was off it was very dark.

Lean   Georgia   Zip

When it came on I asked Lean, "How did the light know when to come on?"

She said, "It was a monkey in that box that over there. That's why they call it the monkey box."

Then I wanted to know, "Who feeds the monkey?"

"We do, but you don't see us for weeks and weeks, I do mean weeks!" She told me.

I told her, "Look like I would be there for some of the times you would be feeding him."

When they found out that I believed them they laughed so hard my Aunt Lean had an accident. I was so sad that they were laughing at me I didn't tell anyone for a whole year.

My Aunt Lean was always playing lots of jokes on me but, I liked it. They weren't there all the time because they had to go sing a lot. They would go with Aunt Lula and others and I would be home with Big Mama and Uncle Luke, Uncle Luke was my step-grandfather, but I didn't know the difference. I loved him the same as any full grandfather.

I didn't like one thing about their life. It was that she had little or nothing, yet she could say nothing about anything. Uncle Luke took care of their son Luke, Jr's every need. She also would hold him close to her and I could see how much she loved her youngest son, too. But to me, Uncle Luke would get jealous of that love, he would call him, to where he was. That was our chance to go and sit next to Big Mama to try and make her feel better.

I always knew she was special. I used to laugh because when I got older and she had so many grandkids that she would call one, she might say Mary, Chan, or Angie before she got to the right name. Then she would say, "You know who I am talking to." We'd laugh not letting her hear us.

I remember when we used to go to Owen Chapel Church, Pastor J. I. Hemphill when she would sing the song "Ninety Nine and A-Half Won't Do, You have to Make one Hundred" that is the song that makes think of her.

Laura, My mother

Angie Mechon Glover

"My Fondest Memories of Grandma"

What I remember most about being at Grandma's, there was always something to do at her house even though there was nothing to do! Each morning everybody would wake up early-- everybody except me. I was always a late morning sleeper. I never got to breakfast on time but, Grandma would always put me a plate up on the stove.

Speaking of breakfast, it was always a hearty meal. We might have things like smothered chicken, biscuits, eggs, homemade pancakes, rice, mind you as I ate it growing up; it was with cream/milk, sugar and buttered, for breakfast. It was a breakfast food for us. It was only later in life when I learned that people ate rice at other meals. You could ask Aunt Elouise about that story. It involved being put out of her house, sitting on a busy street curb waiting for Mom with my sister and brother!

Okay back to Grandma

The summers we spent at Grandma's were more like adventures. We would take long walks, leaving the house in the morning going down a path that kept us occupied in the woods all-day long. Somehow we never got lost, that could remember, because we always found our way out of the woods. Where we came out was not necessarily where we went in. The house was always in sight.

I can remember Grandma making the best tasting blackberry cobbler from the berries we had picked on our wanderings. Not only was it the best tasting treat, but we were so proud to be the procurer of the awesome addition to the meal.

After a long day of wandering in the woods and playing for hours the grandkids would sit on the porch after our baths in her #10 tub and listening to the stories and poems she told all of us throughout the years.

Remembering those evenings sitting there on that porch with Grandma as she shelled purple-hulled peas or snapped beans for the next day's meal just put a smile on my face. I would try and help but I was probably putting more stems in the bowl than actual peas or beans. It was still enjoyable.

Even though we had TV at the time, it was much more exciting to listen as Grandma recited her poems and stories than try and get the antenna just right for a picture on the TV. Watching TV was not an easy task always. Somebody would go outside the house and twist the antenna while someone inside adjusted the rabbit ears with tin foil wrapped around them on the inside of the house. When the picture was finally clear and you took your hands off; we would many times be back at step one of the adjusting process. Eventually, we would either give up or watched a fuzzy picture. One could only get a good picture on a good day every once in a while.

Memories that come to my mind not thought of in years . . . .

- *Wash Day*

Doing the laundry was an entire day's job when one was without a washer and dryer like most folk have today. You couldn't just put clothes into a machine and go on about your business. When I was little Grandma used a "rub board" and the clothes were dried on a clothesline (a long wire or tiny ropelike string line propped up high in the air by poles where clothes were hung to dry). These days a rub board is a cool antique decoration in places like museums or Cracker Barrel's. It is now not a necessity.

Grandma eventually got a washer with a wringer that you had to manually feed the clothes though to wring out the excess water. We had a hose that was connected to a facet over the kitchen sink that was used to put water into the washer when one began and in between the wash and rinse cycle the water had to be drained out and emptied outside. The clothes still had to be hung on the clothesline to be dried.

- *Beauty Shop*

Me/Angie

At Grandma House, the beauty shop was located in the kitchen. I was not one to volunteer to get hair washed, pressed or combed. My favorite words were. "Wait till tomorrow" in the hope tomorrow never would come. When I was small I could crawl upon the counter and hold my head under the facet in the kitchen sink. As I grew older, I would lean over in a chair and she would hold my head under the water in a tub or a pan on the table.

The use of the straightening comb always got me a whipping because I would duck and dodge, which would cause Grandma to burn herself trying not to burn me. Thank God for chemicals!!!

- *Going to Church*

Grandma didn't drive, nor did she have a car, so we would start out walking and eventually someone would pick us up on the way. Once we got to Owens Chapel on Highway 84, we sat on those wooden benches as we listened to her during the services with such enthusiasm. I would sit in church mad because I had had to get my hair combed. I didn't understand her joyful praise at the time. But I and everyone present could tell she was glad to be in church.

- *Her Teacakes*

All I can say is that…. To me, she made the best! I just wish I had learned to make them.

- *The "Slop-jar/Pee-pot" and Out-house experience*

Generations after me will never experience living in a house without indoor bathroom facilities. If you had a weak bladder and couldn't make it the night there was a small white bucket with a lid that that my aunts and uncles called a "Slop-jar" and I called a "Pee-pot". In the mornings someone would has the enjoyable task of emptying it.

However, if you had other business to do during the night, that was a different story. We wake up two or three people because you had to go outside in the dark to the "Outhouse" (the smelly little house out back for that purpose). We would bunch up and quickly make the trip with whomever. The one who went with the person in need would be yelling, "Hurry up, it is scary out here!" I can say it is definitely a luxury to just go down the hall or to the next room, flip the light on and take care of business.

- *The Party Line*

When the phone rang at Grandma's house, it also rang at the neighbor's house. Then you would answer to see who was calling and say "I got it." Everyone else was supposed to hang up. But, the party-line was just that! Your conversation was never private. I know, because we used to sneak and listen to other people on the phone.

- Boys and My First Car

When Grandma moved to Dallas with us, she was my ally. She's the one who was on my side when I wanted to start getting phone calls from boys in the ninth grade. Grandma was also there when I had my very first date.

When I learned how to drive and got a car she was my riding buddy. If I said, "Let's roll," she'd grab her purse and we would be everywhere on any given day. When I learned to drive I learned where every major mall was located in Dallas and the surrounding suburbs.

At first she was probably quite afraid because I was inexperienced and drove rather fast. I would say to her, "Grandma, if you're scared just hold-on to it all. Don't scream out loud." Eventually, she stopped holding on and learned to ride with me and not flinch. Either I started driving better or she got used to my driving. I don't know which it was.

The love she showed and the wisdom that she imparted in us is priceless. Each lesson learned was well taught and never to be forgotten. We experienced so many things that the generations after me will hear or read about. They will never know how it feels to be playing with the chickens in the yard and the next time you see one of them they are smothered in gravy served up with fresh mashed potatoes and green beans.

Life in the country as we lived it with Grandma was too simple compared to today; we enjoyed being *kids* making our own fun.

Grandma, I sure miss you!

Laura, my mother

Chanellon Yvette Jones Williams

"Things I Remember About Grandma"

My sister Angie and I share many memories of Grandma; in fact most of hers are right on point. I was wondering what I could add to what she has already said. Boy am I glad that, I, being a few years older than she, and our brother Clarence, I have a few more thoughts of my own to add

Clarence Jones

One of the first things I remember about Grandma was, at Grandma's house you did **not** play any kind of cards, dominos, or checkers. None of them were ever in her house.

Before I was old enough to hang out in the woods, each day breakfast was followed by no less than two hours of prayer and meditation with the Lord. Every day I would listen to Grandma as she talked to the Lord about family, loved ones, friends, neighbors and the nation. Yes the nation.

As a child, I was totally confused by the process....same time, same place, same conversation. I would whine and remind Grandma that we were here yesterday and told Him the same thing, then I would ask, "Why do we gotta' keep telling Him the same thing over and over?" She would call it 'storing up timber!' She never changed.

I remember my getting my hair done by Grandma out under the trees in the yard. I don't remember going through the drama my sister Angie went through.

Grandma taught me how to cook. My being left-handed posed a major challenge for everyone else including my mother. They would always say that I looked like I was going to drop everything but, not Grandma. She never mentioned it. She taught me well and I love cooking to this day. She taught me to make pot-luck stew with hot links....yum. Shameful that no one else in the family learned her recipe.

I remember going to church with Grandma. I fact if you were in Grandma's house on Sunday church you were expected to attend or you had to be sick. Well, my memory of her at church was singing a song called "Rock Daniel" (What cha' come here for?) there. She would sing until the power of the Lord filled the building. She was faithful and filled with the Spirit.

I remember that when we were walking to church I didn't do it as quietly as Angie and Clarence did. I had questions. Grandma would always want us to start out **walking**. Since she would tell us that God knows all about us and He would provide. My question was ALWAYS.... "Since He knows, why can't He provide BERORE we start walking?" To me it was a totally confusing process. But, she never changed, as far as she was concerned God would always provide.

Grandma was the first person that I ever heard quote the phrase, "Forgit cha,' forgot cha' I never thought about cha'."

She was a Godly woman. While she could never teach me to be quiet, there are so many other things she not only taught me but, lived a daily example of unwavering strength, steadfast in prayer and faith in God. I had no idea back then that a foundation was being laid inside of me that would carry me through many things years into the future.

I even memorized the ending she used most of the time when she prayed I heard her pray so often. It goes this way....

"....And when all have fought the battle of life;

When it comes yours to call; and ours to go;

We pray for a peaceful quiet hour in death

And heaven receive our souls is our honest prayer."

I stand with victory in my life on top of "timber" stored up by my Grandmother

Eddie, my Mother

Kenneth Wayne Durham

My Grandmother; a Special Woman

My Grandmother was a special woman. Although she was blessed with more than a handful of grandchildren she could make each one of us feel as if we were the only one she had. I always felt that way!

She possessed a quiet inner strength that as a child I didn't understand. But, now as an adult I know it to be her faith and strength in the Lord. I never remember her being mad outwardly but once. I could always tell what kind of mood she was in by tone of her humming, which it seemed she did most of the time that I could remember. If the melody was upbeat and cheerful so was she. If the hymn was reserved, slow and despairingly I always felt like she was in deep thought about something. I used to love to hear it either way. It made me feel good for some reason.

I used to look forward to her fried chicken it always tasted so good even though I watched her prepare it there was always the slightest amount of shortening on the pan. It amazed me how she would make each piece so evenly golden brown and evenly cooked when there was never enough oil to cover the pieces.

As an adult I have burned or oven cooked many a piece of chicken trying to do it the way she used to.

She always seemed very busy, be it washing, hanging up clothes, cooking or sewing a quilt. The quilts she made were also a work of art. There was always one there to admire. The quilts were made from small pieces of cloth, leftover material from sewing or old worn out clothes of cotton and corduroy that had good parts left. I used to think it was so difficult especially since the quilts were made of utility weight fabric of bright colors or floral print. I liked the corded ones the best because they were snot so "fu fu" as most of the others.

She must have known I liked that kind because when I grew older and graduated from high school was headed off to college she gave me the kind of quilt. She told me as she gave it to me, 'It might get cold."

That was 30 cold years ago and it still keeps me warm to this day!

The one time I did see Grandma kinda' mad was my doing. I was at her house where there was a large propane tank that stood off to one side. I was rounded like the mid section of a horse but, it sat up off the ground a good bit. If a kid was on it and slipped of it would make for a nasty fall.

To me it looked like an imaginary horse that was beginning to be roped, so one day I figured out a way to get up on it and finally fulfill "it's" wish to be roped.

After having my wild cowboy adventure I remember going back into the house and she met me at the door. She asked me had I been on top of the tank. I could tell just by her tone that it probably wasn't going to be a wise choice to admit I had been so I said, "No Ma'am."

Bad move!

Little did I realize that because the tank was outside in the hot Texas summer sun, the white paint that covered the tank by then had a rather chalky composition? That small oversight on my part cost me. What I also didn't notice was that my pants were covered in the white chalky paint.

That chased away my luck big time!

My sweet loving grandmamma gave me a switching that 40 plus years later, I don't feel I will ever forget.

As I mentioned earlier she made everyone of her grandchildren feel as if they were the only one she had. I remember how special the beds were in Grandmother's house, I mention the beds because she didn't have any fancy heating system in her house. The only heating in the house was in the front bedroom or the room where Grandmother and Uncle Luke slept and where everyone usually gathered. It was her version of a "Family room" that had a wood stove, I have no idea why you called it that, maybe, because you did not cook on it, it was just there to keep things warm.

The room where I usually slept was a bit off from that room. The East Texas winters could sometimes get quite cold during the night but, it never mattered because of my Grandmother's beds. She had these big feather stuffed mattresses that you could sink down into. She would then load several of her quilts on top of you and you'd be set for the night. It wouldn't matter how cold it got you would never know it, you couldn't even move! I don't know if it was feather mattress that I sunk into or all the quilts, but I do remember waking up many mornings in the exact position I went to sleep in the night before. I would be contented and rested. It was real cool!

All these memories of Grandmother are so comforting, and as well as the feeling she gave all of us that each, one of us, were very special to her.

Grandmother was a special lady!

Eddie, my mother

Bobby Jean Durham, Junior

She Was My Grandma, Too!

There are things about being in Grandma's company that linger with me. The first thing is that she used to live in the country and my visiting there was so much fun. Not to mention that she would always make me feel special!

I can remember when we were there and Grandma made coffee for Uncle Luke. She had a special kind of pot that she used. I even have one that reminds me of it. When Uncle Luke poured his coffee into his cup he would overfill it so that it would run into the saucer then Uncle Luke would drink it from the saucer.

Grandma was also famous for her special teacakes! She even allowed some of us grandchildren to help her make them on occasion. We were given a cup to use as the cutters to cut the teacakes for baking. She even let us do it on her birthday, as seen below after we finished.

Me and some of my cousins with Grandma on her birthday
Wilbur Delaney Wright, Grandma, Michele Jones, Renee`, Diron Charles, me,
Cindy, Byron, and the little guy is Cedric

By the time I came along she let me do a few things she would not let the other grand- children do. I was allowed to wonder in the woods alone. I even got my only, whipping from her, because I took some of the other children on the tour of the woods with me. Some of them were older than me, but they were not allowed in the woods.

I got to like hunting and guns at Grandma's. Uncle Luke would let me see his guns and even let try shooting one of them.

At Grandma's everyone had things to do. We all had to pick and shell peas. I even had the experience of helping Uncle Luke feed the hogs. We picked wild plums that Grandma made into the very delicious tasting preserves.

She was good grandma to all of us.

I was glad that my son to meet her even though he may not remember it I have a picture to show him that he took with his great- grandmother taken when she had reach a tender age. She and Josh like some of the same items.

She was also so glad to see him. It brightened up her day so much when we took him by to see her even when she had not being feeling too well during her last days.

He always tried to take her can and her juice. She never seemed to mind because she would always continue to smile and hug him.

Grandma and Joshua Blake

Grandma was one who liked to be involved in things she also was one who liked to travel as she did with my parents and other members of the family. As others noted she was one for worshiping God.

These were some of the things I remember of my Grandmother!

Evelyn, my mother

Carolyn Ann Jones-Bartlett

Grandma

My first memories of Grandma were of when I might have been about 5 or 6. It was a spring day and the cows were loose in the fields and Grandma told me to stay close to the house, but me being the person I was, wanted to see what was going on. Uncle Luke was in the field so I wanted to see what was happening. One of the cows, a bull turned and started chasing me! I was wearing red. Grandma was in the kitchen she standing near the sink and looked out of the window. She saw me running screaming my head off, with the bull chasing me. She came running out of the house taking her apron off at the same time. As she came along side me she wrapped the apron around me. We made it to the house unscathed and, I then learn that bulls did not like red!

Carolyn, Mama and Luke Junior dressed for church

Thinking back on the times I spent with her what I noticed that impacted me was she was always a very quiet, spiritual person. When things upset her she would always pray. She never raised her voice. I remember this one time when Grandma 'put a church' at the front door. She would sit there as she prayed most of the day.

I don't know what caused the action but I do remember that I was scared to go out that door!

Grandma raised us in church. On our way to church we walked liked baby ducks following our mother. We would stay in church; it seemed like, all day. We dared not complain though. Even at a young age she instilled spiritual growth in us, and for which I am thankful for today.

Junior and Carolyn

I stayed with Grandma until 1959, when I moved to California. I grew up there and remained there until January, 1997. The thing about that is I had always said that I would never come back to Texas to live. After a visit in August of 1996 I decided then that it was time to come back home. I am thankful to God for bringing me home because it gave me the chance to have some quality time with Grandma.

Since I have been here in Dallas Aunt Georgia has become pastor of the church where Grandma and the family would go. She sat beside me during the service and would not let anyone else sit beside her. During her last months, Grandma, would most of the time, come into the church pushing her walker saying "huka-a –daddy, huka-a daddy". Those were signs that she was having a bad day. On those days she did not want to be bothered.

A while later during the service she would say "That girl needs to be quiet (speaking of Pastor Georgia). She's been talking too long!" She would then attempt to get up and leave, most of the times she got her way.

Grandma at the church sitting in the pastor's chair on her 97ᵗʰ birthday

I am thankful for the time that I got to spend with Grandma. She will be in my heart and life forever. Grandma raised her children, grandchildren and great grandchildren all six generations the way Proverbs 31:10 speak of the virtuous woman. Grandma was truly a virtuous woman. The Bible tells us to train up a child in the way he ought to go and when he is older he will not depart from it. That is what Grandma did for her family.

Grandma kept us in God's hands

Georgia, my mother

ILA Michelle Kilgore

Grandma

There are not enough good words that I could say about my sweet loving Grandma. She was an inspiration to all of us. I loved her so much, and she will always have a large part of my heart.

I can remember back when I was small, how no matter how many children were around she made each of us feel like we were the special one. There were many a summer I spent with her and Uncle Luke (Grandpa) that I will **never** forget.

Though she was a loving person, she never had a problem with disciplining me when I was wrong!

There was a summer that I remember when my sister Cindy, my cousins, Keena and Tamiko were with me at Grandma and we liked to play a card game called UNO when we wanted to amuse ourselves when we were not pulling peas, looking for berries or fishing. She didn't like our playing any kind of cards. She didn't make us stop our playing this one but, I can remember it like it was yesterday when Grandma went around saying UNO, UNO, UNO over and over again.

Grandma's cooking was the best ever! I loved everything about it. I just looked forward to getting up in the mornings there to see what we were going to eat for breakfast. She would always make it smell so good.

Grandma

After I got to be an adult I got a chance to be around Grandma, morning, noon and night and she still had a way of making everyone feel important!

When I came home even late at night, she would most of the time be up waiting for me, and many times she would even have something for me to eat.

I cannot express the strong feelings I felt for my Grandma. I was so very proud to be her granddaughter.

She was a praying, Blessed Woman of God. She taught all of us to love God like never before. I see others families in the world that are not nearly as deeply rooted in The Word of God as ours have always been. We have all strayed away, a time or two we knew where we should get back to. Not saying our family is perfect by any means but, she taught all of us that God gives second chances. When we come to ourselves, we need to confess our sins to God, and ask Him for forgiveness. He is there!

To be a woman that has roots from Grandma is a blessing. It has taught me that I need to be strong Black woman no matter what.

To have had a chance to have had Grandmother as long as we did I must thank God for being so kind. Not many are 97 years blessed as we were!

Grandma, I love and miss you. I hope in heaven, you are sharing all of your beautiful poems you shared with us. I will never forget you or what you taught me. I hope to make you proud of me as I was so very proud and honored to be a part of you!

Venus Lean, My mother

Tommy Lenard (Peezy) Bridges

"Grandma Babe"

Everlena Hayes Weaver Jones Durham, or as I knew her, Grandma Babe, was a great lady to be around. I can say I have fond memories connected with her from my childhood until her untimely death. My mother Venus Lean Jones Bridges was the youngest of her daughters. Mom would tell us, my brothers and me how it was growing up in Grandma Babe's house. Now that she and my mother are together with all the other family members who have already gone on my, brothers and reminisce back to time when they were here and we were with Grandma Babe.

Growing up Granny knew me as Peezy. I am the youngest of Lean's boys, Tommie Bridges, Jr. My two older brothers are Wilbur Delaney and Diron Charles Jones. What I can remember of my Granny was going to her house in Fairfield (Butler), Texas during the summer vacation. I would play with Byron and Cedric because we were within the same age group or range.

While Granny was fixing breakfast we would be playing. What a breakfast it usually was! It was usually between about 7 and 8 o'clock in the morning. Whatever she served us was always very good and we all had enough. Uncle Luke Her late husband had a personal pot filled with well water. I got into trouble because I would decide to drink from his pot. That was a lesson learned.

He passed away around my eleventh birthday but she would have us down until the following year. She moved in with Aunt Laura (Shug, to us) house in Dallas. She remained there until her "Leave of Absence."

When she came to live there, I would go there to see her there every time we went with Mom to Aunt Shug's house. She would be in the family room reading her Bible. Many times she would be in the kitchen fixing her very good tasting teacakes. Yeah teacakes,

Grandma' homemade teacakes were a family favorite. She would also give me ginger snaps.

Every Sunday while she was going to True Way Church of God in Christ she was there. I would sit by her (My mother was a musician and was usually in the choir stand), and Grammy would give me an orange candy slice or a piece of peppermint when/if I acted up to calm me down.

I didn't get in trouble much with Grandma Babe. She always made me feel good.

As time went by, and I got older I would still visit Aunt Shug's house and she would still be in the family room reading her Bible or watching TBN. We would spend time talking to each other.

I can truly say that she was a fair woman. She never had a favorite for she loved us all the same. My father Tommy, Sr. would always ask about her after one of my visits with her even though he and my mom were not together.

My mom died and I took it quite hard but Grandma Babe held strong for me and her.

She was a very strong woman. I thank her for helping me through all of the motherless holidays after Mom died. She was a fine Granny.

I miss here as I know everyone in the family does, but she is still with me giving me her blessing. She brings me calm instead of orange candy slices and peppermints.

I am proud to have the opportunity to say some things about my
beloved Grandma Babe, God Bless!

Georgia, My mother

Recenda "Cindy" Ellis

Grandmama's Story

Where do I begin? I remember so many different things about Grandmama. The one thing that stands out the most for me right now would be our going out together on Saturdays. Before her health got so bad I would pick her up on Saturday's and take her shopping for the little "what knots" she wanted. Many of the times, of course she would get some of the things she really needed as well. We would try to most or our outing for as long as she could stand it. Through it all we had so much fun.

After our shopping tour of stores our together fun times was spent at Chuck E Cheese! Yes I know, why, you ask would she always wanted to go there?

She enjoyed watching the children play and there was a stage where funny looking characters were singing. After the many trips to Chuck E Cheese on Saturdays, one Tuesday afternoon she had the family frantic!

That day Grandmama thought it was Saturday and that she had waited and waited on me to come and get her. I didn't come. She thought that she would just get her a ride to Chuck E Cheese and meet me there. Needless to say, I was not there, because it was on a Tuesday I was at work. I got this call from my mother that told me that Grandmama was missing!

After hours of looking for her through the neighborhood, posting signs around and talking with the police they had no luck finding her. I drove home to meet the rest of the family. On my way there I thought where she might have gone. I got my phone, called Mama and told her to have someone meet me at the Chuck E Cheese were usually went to. I thought that was where she would go.

We arrived there at about the same time, went in. There we found her just as happy and jolly as could be. She was sitting at the table watching the children there in the place. We asked her how she was able to get to the place. Her answer was that some nice little boy brought her.

Or course that brought a storm of questions from the police who had been looking for her all around the area near my Aunt Evelyn's home and other parts of the city since she had been gone so long. We were upset and lad to have found her but puzzled at the actions she seemed to be unfazed about. She was just glad to have had a chance to go to Chuck E Cheese.

Her lovely smile would pop up whenever anyone would mention the escapade she went on that day to her.